I0755767

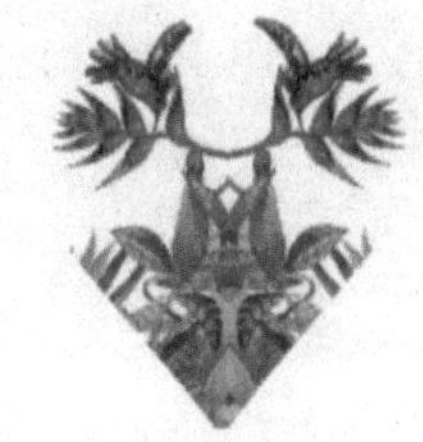

**tpprince esquire international**

2016

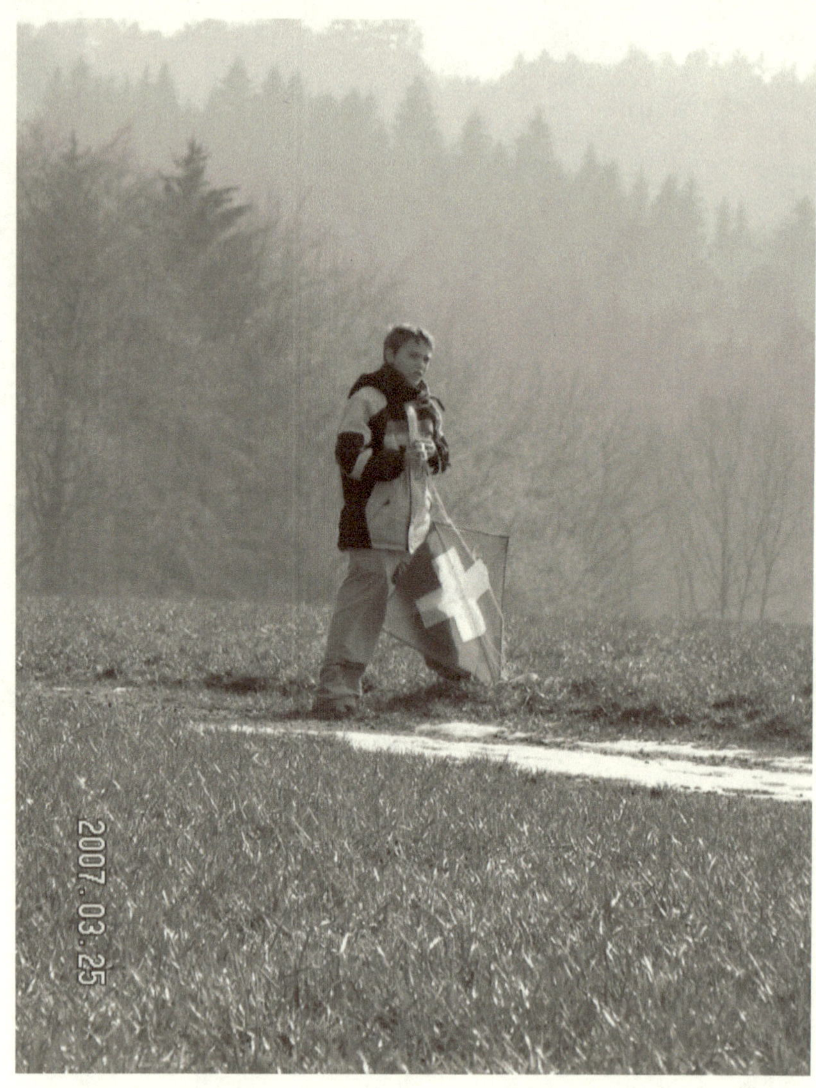
2007.03.25

# TESTING THE AUTUMN BREEZE 2016

ISBN: 978-0-9790110-9-2

***POEMS, ILLUSTRATIONS AND FRIENDS***

***A collected effort of tpprince and unmitigated Blindness***

*BY* **Daniel Sekarski alias tpprince**

Published and Copyrighted
**tpprince esquire international**
St. Louis U.S.A Froideville Switzerland
2010

*Profits from this book are to be used to support a non-profit children's publishing effort :*
**tpprince esquire international**
**San 852-2219**

**Reprints:**
**http://stores.lulu.com/tpprince_esquire**
**Email tpprince@tpprince-esquire.com**
**Web page http://tpprince-esquire.com**

*A life in poems cannot be dedicated to any single person. It can only be dedicated to all the people, all the experiences and all the privileges that a life time of blindness and self absorption can excrete. We can mentions the ones who stand out in our minds but these are not usually the true shapers of our aimless existence. It is often the people we never saw, never really met, and never really acknowledged who made our life what it is.*

*The man who stopped the car and didn't run you over when you hurriedly rode your bike across the street without looking, the women who kept you safe when you were too daring or too stupid to consider the consequences of your childish actions, the stranger who stayed with you when you were a completely hopeless asshole or too drunk to safely function, the friend who held the mirror in front of you so you could see yourself for the inconsiderate jackass that you were being, the lover who left you in the dust when she knew it was time for her to go, or the one who stayed at great personal cost in order to fulfil the need you had but could not admit to.*

*Our lives are pieced together with the spit, sweat and tears of a universe of caring and uncaring people who pass in a constantly expanding spiral surrounding our narrow vision of the world we think we live in.*

# Testing the Autumn Breeze

*Poems, Illustrations and friends*

*A collected effort of T.P.Prince and unmitigated Blindness*

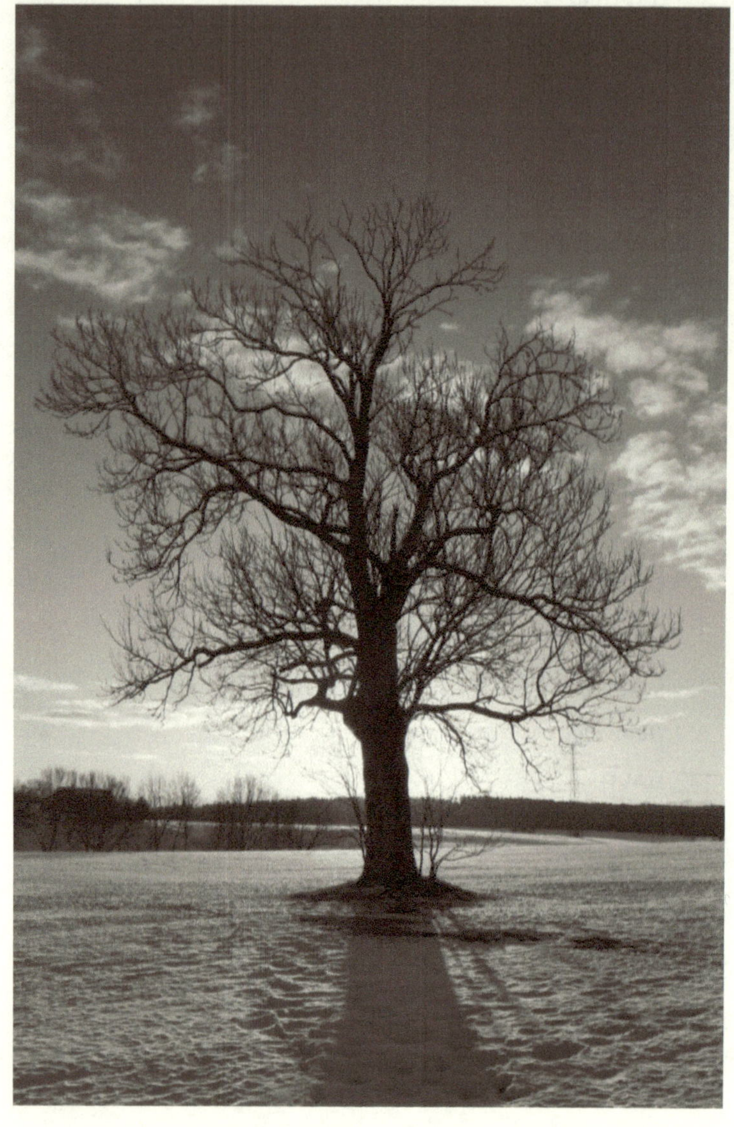

# *testing the autumn breeze*

As the autumn breezes
whip the thinning hair on balding heads
we finally begin to look around.

Looking back-------
we forget to look up

we see out lives----
---------drifting
out of ----------reach
out of ---------touch
of ---------bounds
--------time.

We become------------
-------cautious
instead of curious
-----------doubtful
instead of hopeful
---------complacent
instead of committed
-----------afraid
instead of daring.

We see winter baring down
Muscles failing
Weight shifting
Minds slipping.

Above us -----------
------------the kites are flying
-------birds are gathering
Clouds are moulding into castles
Life is preparing ----
----------for the next spring

Children testing ---------
their abilities
--------------to soar
-----------------to glide

---------- to dive
------- to reach new heights
the winds blow-------
-----------in their faces
pulling against their strings
raising them up
to places -------------
they have never been
---------before
and-------------- may never find
-------again.

As our eyes begin
-------------to fail
We finally
--------------begin to see.

T. P. Prince

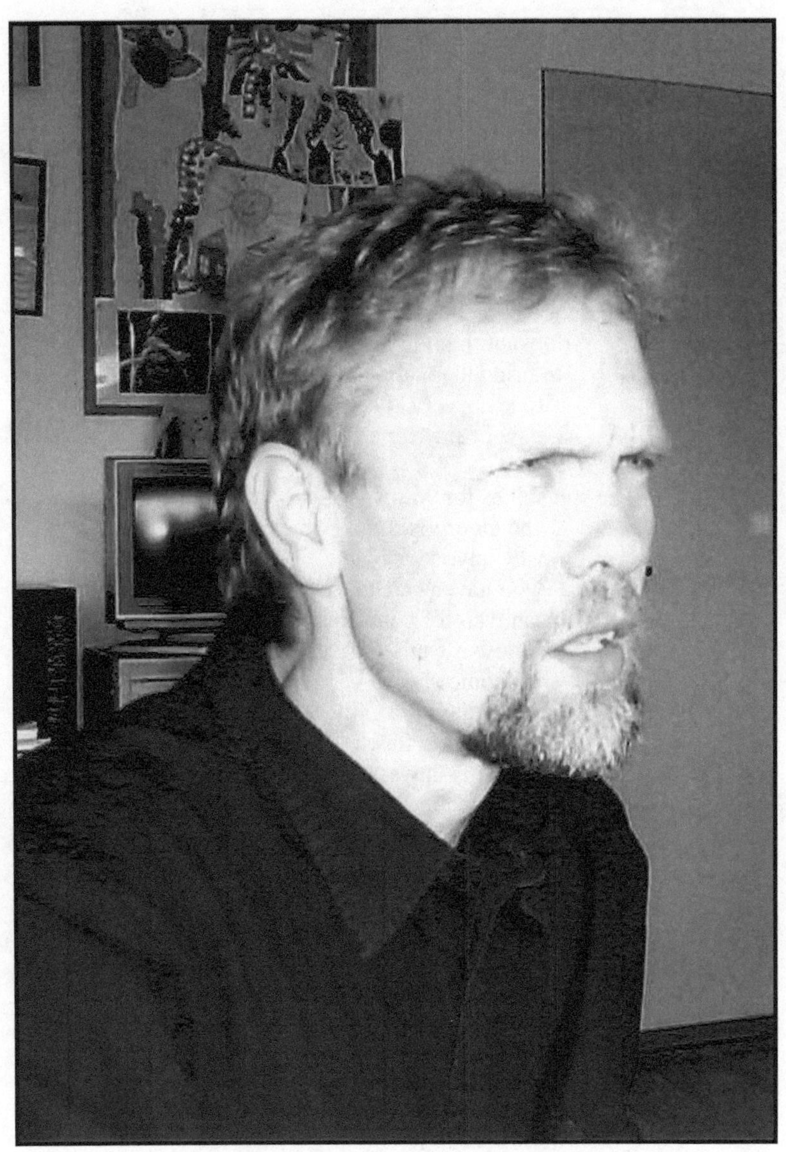

Author tpprince

# don't bug me

Some days-----------------------------
the world glows to your touch
the breeze carries you like a kite
the bugs never bite
the worst pains become light

People are beautiful---------------------
you want to know them all
to bring them all home
to kiss every cheek
have them stay for a week

The sun shines for you----------------
the moon rises too
why anyone is blue
you haven't a clue
you can wait for your dream
you know it waits for you
somewhere
where the days are endless
the nights are flawless
love is lawless
and can redeem
everything that was
ever lost

The dream has survived-----------
the forced rapes
the brutal torture
the constant neglect
the careless lies
your inability to respond

even if
you should die
the dream will survive
the birches will be bent to the ground

by the storm
but they will not break
they will not up-root
they will not be
eradicated

There is a power---------------------
that will not be denied
there is a song
that can not be forgotten
there is a memory
that forever binds us
together
for all time
in all places
with every caring touch
every kind word
with every gentle breath.

T. P. Prince

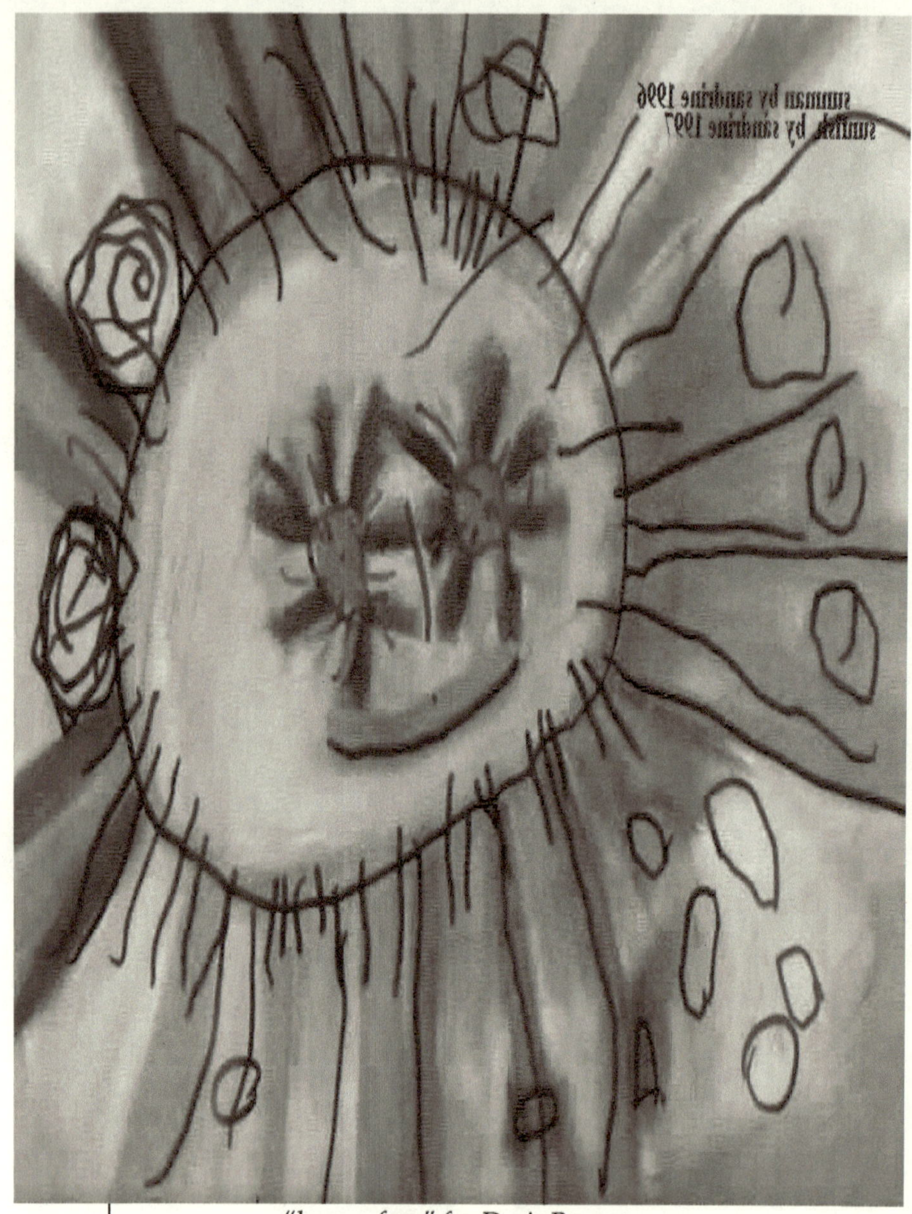


"happy face" for Doris Brown

# Feet of clay

The future will find us..
In places we never ....

Amid times we had thought ....
We were prepared for
Doing things we never dreamed
We might have to do

But today......

The future smiles
With bright eyes
Reaching for stars
With tiny fumbling hands
And feet of clay

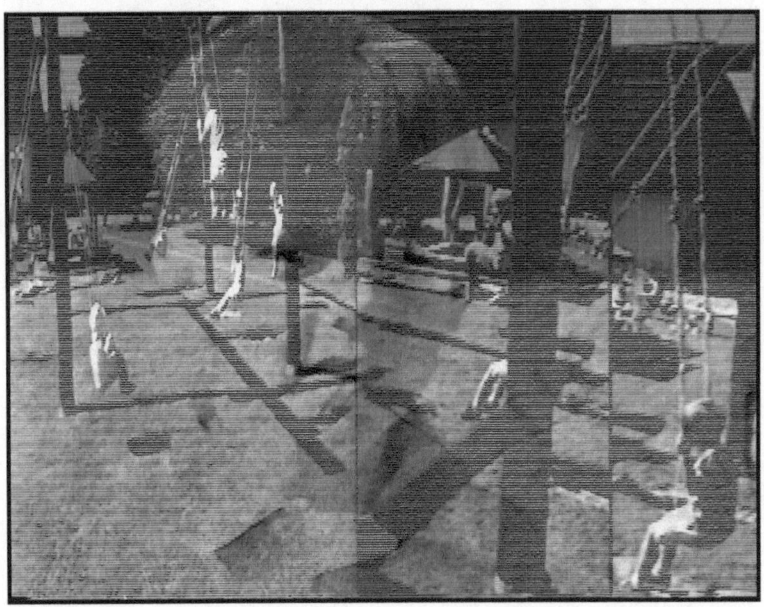

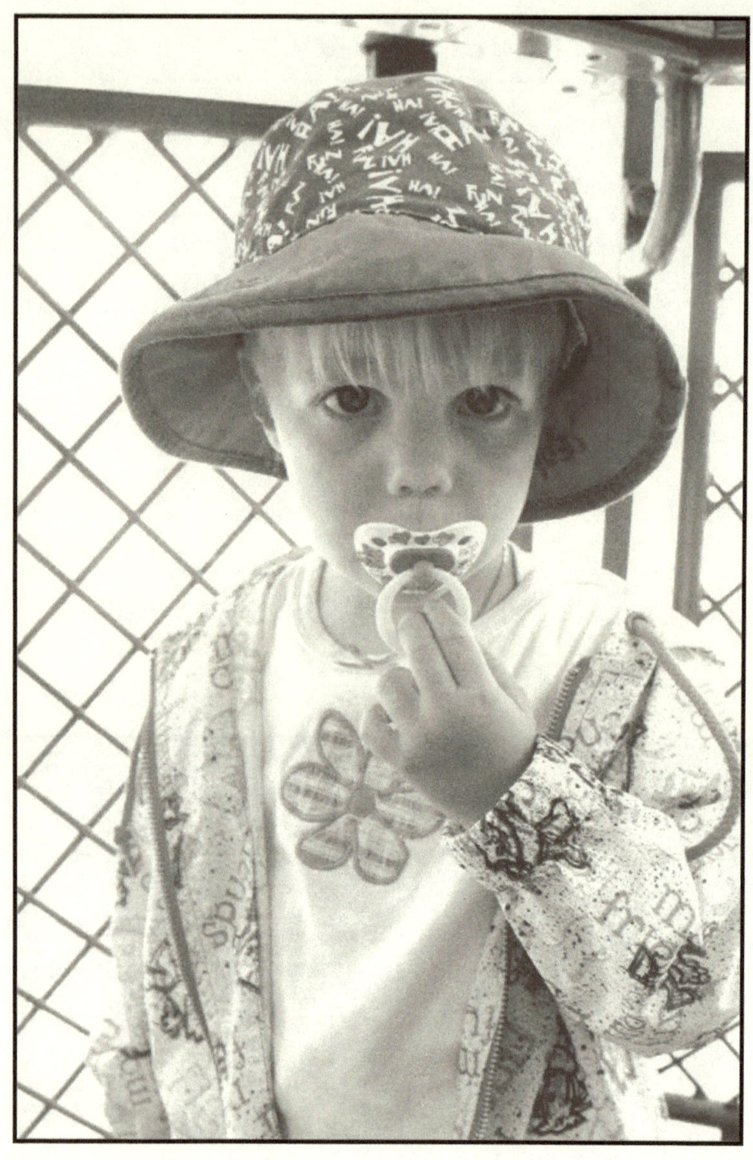

# Growin'

turn and run--------------------
from the frightening changes

growin' up
for what?
growin' old
it's been fortold
age grey
but don't get serious
stay close to us

remember-
if you can

the touch of a hand
the battles of Pan
the curve of the land
the breath of a woman
the scent of a sleeping infant
safe and happy
in your arms
as the sun slowly fades
behind the curve
leaving shadows on walls
ghosts in the halls

as it all fades into night--
whisper your prayer
put the child to bed
pull the cover over your head
forget all that was said
rest your cheek
on the softness of the child's forehead
feel the Spirit
he remains with the child
as the child remains

forever----------------
with the man.

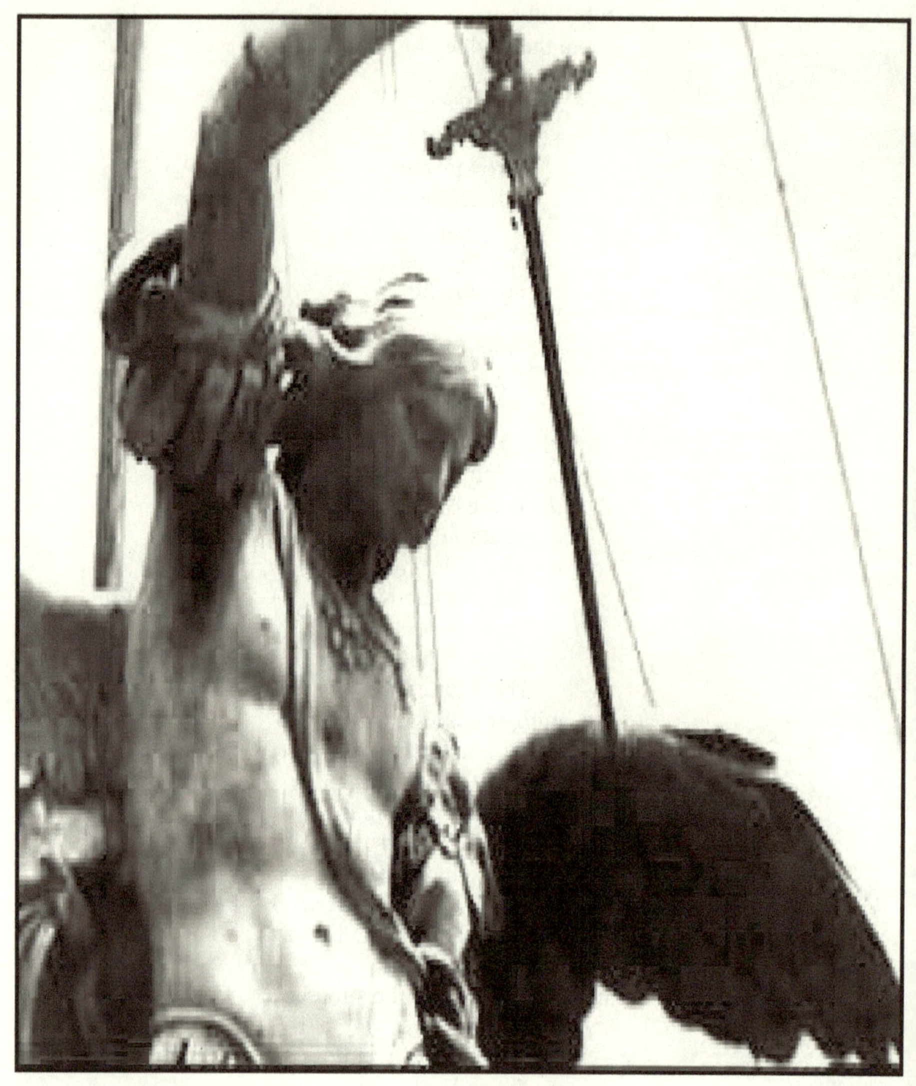

*The arch-angle St. Michael  Vatican City*

# Kosovo

Is it wise-----------
to believe
to trust
to love

is it wise----------
to speak when not sure
to hear but not listen
to touch and not feel

is it wise----------
to see and not care
to empathize and not help
to forget and not forgive

is it wise-----------
to believe and not understand
to long for with no hope
to go on, with no place to go.

is it wise----------
to give away one's heart
to sacrifice one's life
to risk one's very soul.

the butterfly gently rises up-------------------
into the mouth
of a waiting swallow
later caught and tortured
by a curious cat
while her young cry out
in wait for her
at the nest.
A man places the cat
in a sack
tossing him into the river
like a twig.

the pegnant cat
will have no kittens----------
The chirping birds
die in the nest
the flowers
lose a friend
the man
kisses his children
The children
search for thier missing pet.

the graves are shallow------------------------
The bodies underneath
rot
the loved ones above
weep
the soldiers
laugh uneasily
as thier souls gently rise up
into the mouth of a waiting swallow.

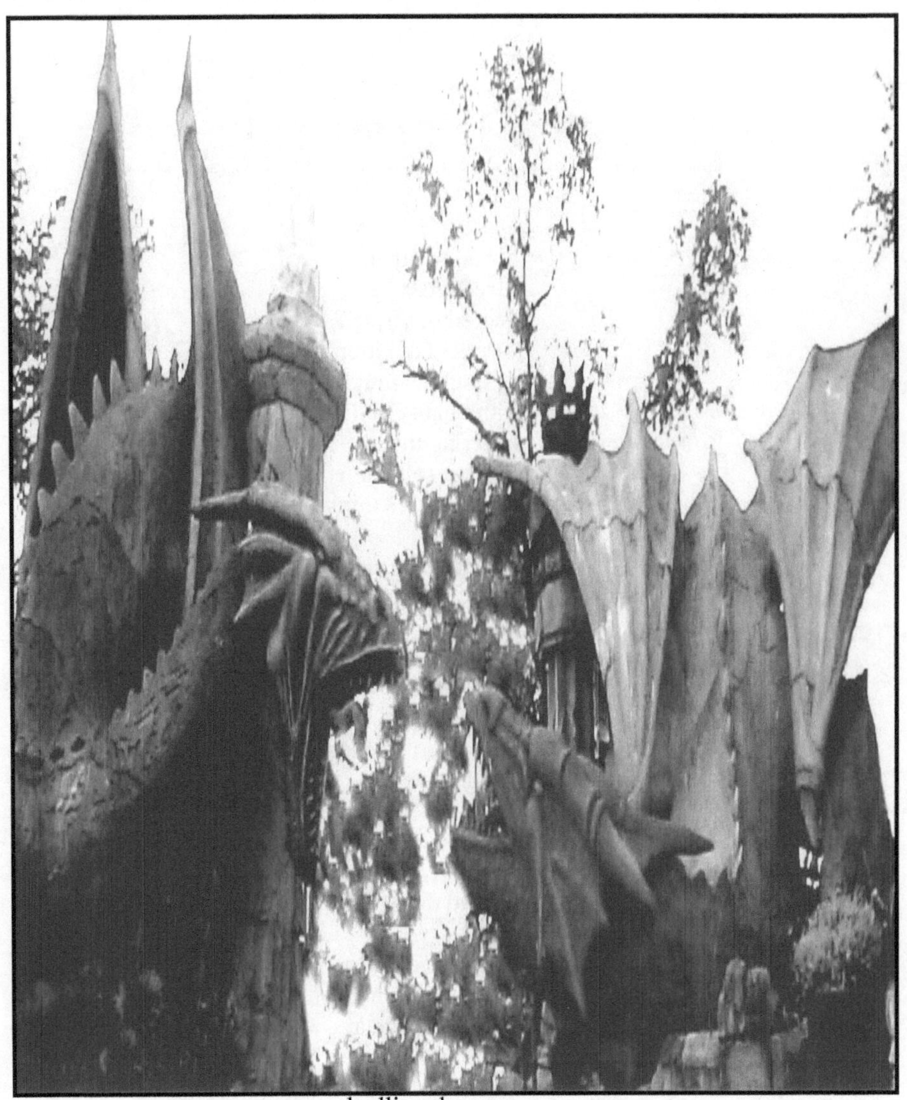

duelling dragons

# Spirit in remission

hating others
reflects a new
hatred of oneself
or ones condition
filling the mind
with muddy malice
covering the heart
with false self centered
rational negative thinking

because of you
there is unhappiness
mistrust
lies
deceit

You have poisoned
my world
raped
my wife
turned my children
to drugs

You have given
weapons to the innocent
pointed them at
existence
pointed them at
providence
urging them to
pull the trigger

You have killed
the messenger
shot
the golden goose

executed
the redeemer.

You have negotiated a place
central in my heart
from there you are able
to touch
to grope
to direct
to controle
my very core.

I thought
we were friends
you guided me
nurtured me
exalted me
then
stripped me
of my pride
my youth
my compassion
my smile.

The rode back…
is impossible
but to stay
is suicide.

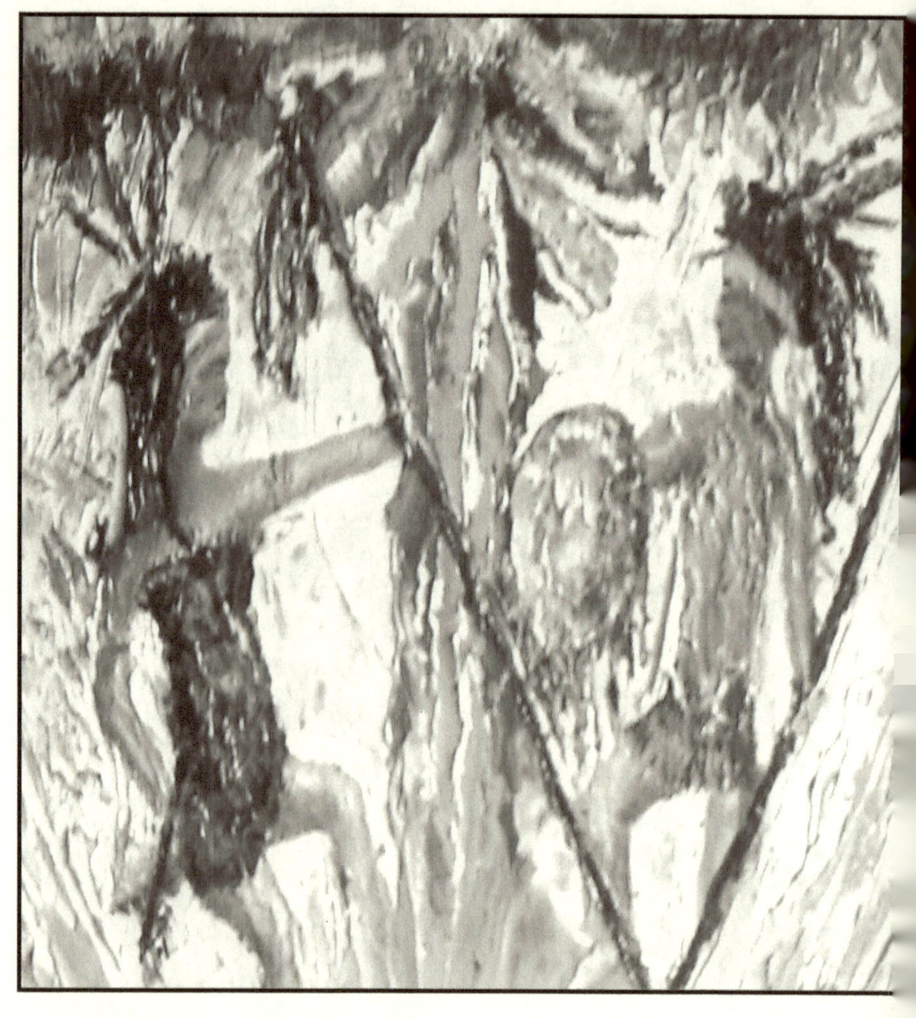

*nouveau monde  tpprince 1993*

# tomorrows end

when one has more to look back on
than to look forward too
the stakes of the game
smack you in the face
like a squeaky clean glass door
that you thought you left open.

the cool slowness of
having all the time in the world
turns into
the savage beast at your back.
like a pacman chasing you
trying to eat you
before you can finish
the thousand projects
that you have been saving in your mind
for a time like this when you thought
you would have all the time in the world

Yes.. you may have more time
but
you have less energy
less ambition
less drive
and less will power.
you want to rest now
the struggle was long and often quite hard
the television is your restful friend
but also your worst enemy.
these nice things that soothe your minds
rob your fleeting desire
and steal your last remnants of time.
but there is always tomorrow!
I will do better tomorrow.

tomorrows end
with a date on your tomb stone.

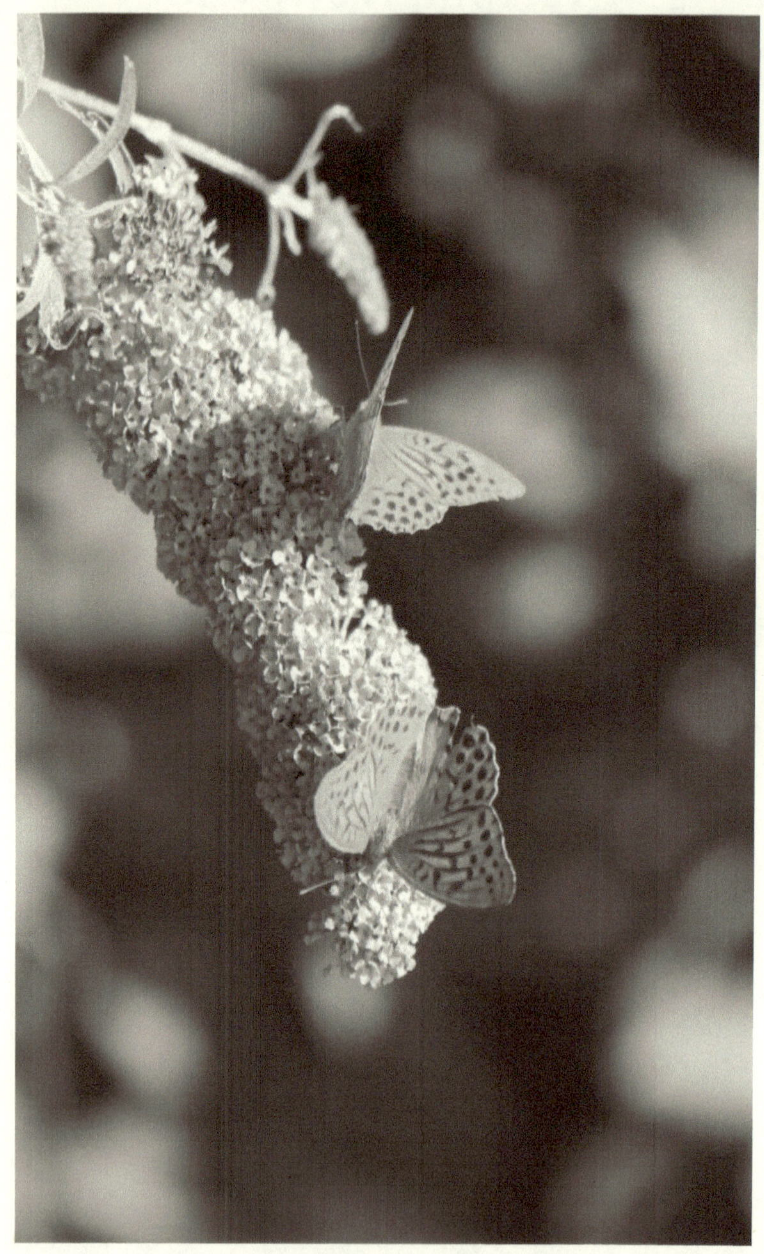

# Why do you stand here?

*I stand here in wonder.......*
*I stand here in fear*
*I stand here in truth*
*I stand here for you.*

*I stand here because.......*
*you stand beside me----*
*sharing your hopes.....*
*entrusting your future.*
*God has guided me here.*

*I don't know if I understand.....*
*all the glitter,*
*all the show;*
*the full pews; the colorful stage.....*
*the smiling faces:*
*the nervous glances.................*
*But I do know that........*
*I love you.*
*I know the simple intimate reality of that.*

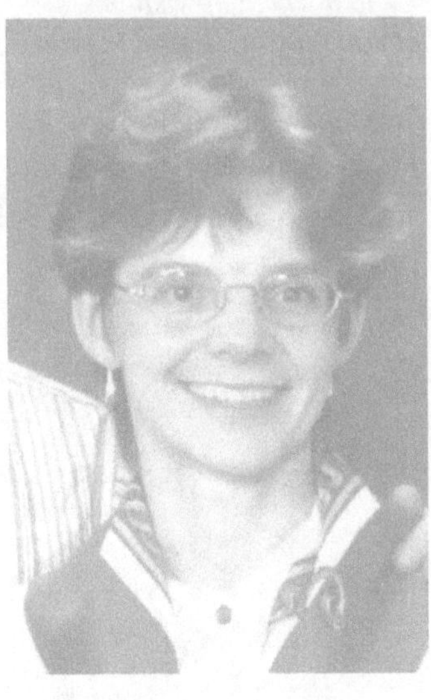

*That is why I stand here,*
*before God*
*before you,*
*before everything that I know*
*before everything that I love.*
*and there is so much*
*that I love......*
*but there is so little*
*that I know.*

*As I stand with you now....*
*I will stand by you always;*
*be it here inh tis church,*
*be it poor and far away.*
*be it in laughter*
*be it surrounded by tears*
*As I stand by you now.........*
*will I stand by you always.*

*Take my hand that we might pass together*
*through the tests of time,*
*across the falls of faith,*
*above the seas of selfishness*
*to a world of wisdom*
*that can only be shared in twos.*

*Why stand you here with me ?*

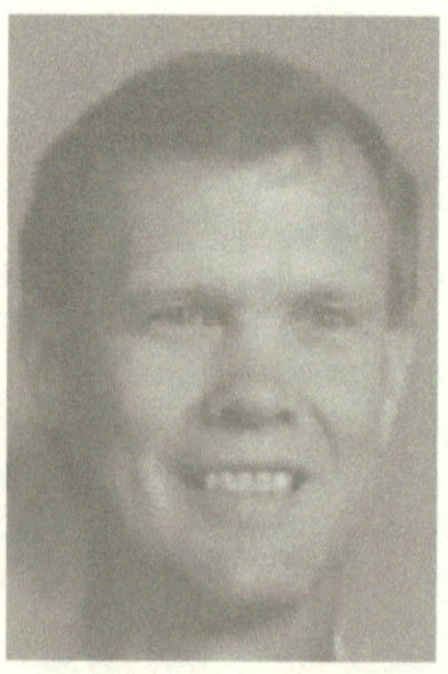

***Everyone's eyes are on me.......***

*I look at the priest, his eyes are so bright,*
*I look at you, you are truly beautiful.*
*by the grace of God.....*
*I do love you;*
*I do need you.*

*I stand here..................*
*that we might stand together;*
*that we might share our dreams.*
*not just today*
*this single day in a string of 25,550 days*
*not just tomorrow*
*the 10,000 tomorrows that we have left*
*But beyond these church walls*
*beyond the light years of measured time*
*Past the pains, the thoughtless games,*
*the many stained glass windows of life*
*Beyond selfish expectations*
*through self-indulgences.*
*Into the morning rays of understanding*
*not only understanding each other*
*but understanding of ourselves.*
*That is why I stand here,*
*before God*
*before you,*
*before everyone that I know*
*before everything that I love.*
*and there is so much*
*that I love......*
*but so little*
*that I know.*
*As I stand by you now....*
*I will stand by you always;*
*be it poor and far away....*
*be it in laughter...*
*be it surrounded by tears.*
*as I stand by you now....*
*I will stand by you always.*

*Take my hand that we might stand together*
*through the tests of time*

*across*
*the falls of faith,*
*above the seas of selfishness*
*t*
*o a world of wisdom*

*that can only be shared by two.*

*Shared*
*by me and you.*

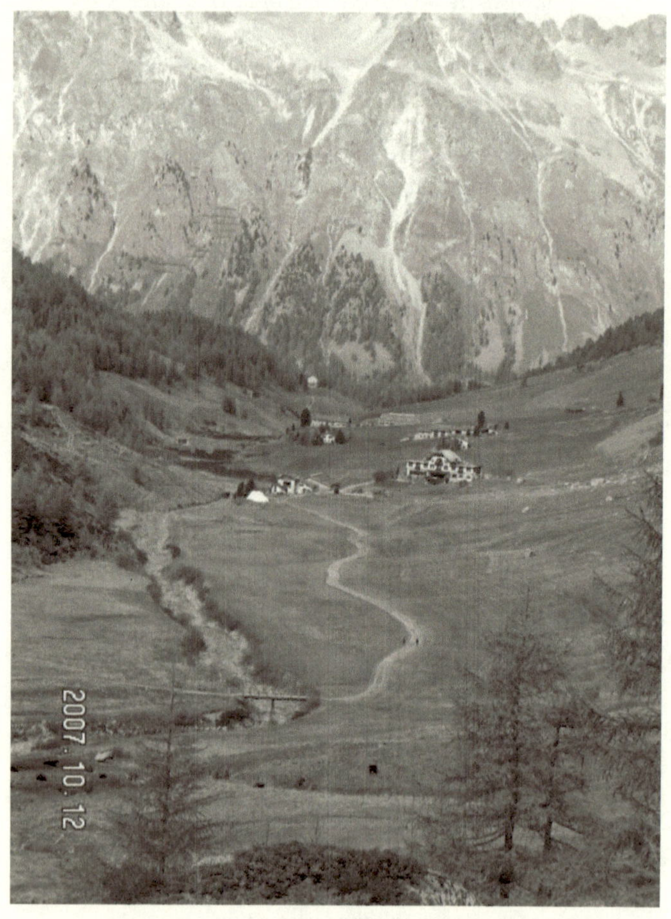

# Sometimes

As one stares out----
across scattered skies
saturated with rain---fog
one feels the chill and damp
and imagines-----

huge clifs of dispair---
tall insurmountable peaks
beyond them----
nothing
but cold ,blue ice
wind hardened snow.

life looks
baren and bleak---
hopeless.

but-----
if one would only
turn slighlty
to the left
the right
to the rear
one might see
the flowers blooming
the children playing
family smiling
friends laughing

one does not need
to
concuer mountains
win at love
put the world at peace
to find himself

----this would be easy

to find happiness
to create the peace

one must---

scale ….
the naked peaks
towering in his own mind
get lost ….
in the crevaces
where love hides .
in the deep reaches….
of our own hearts

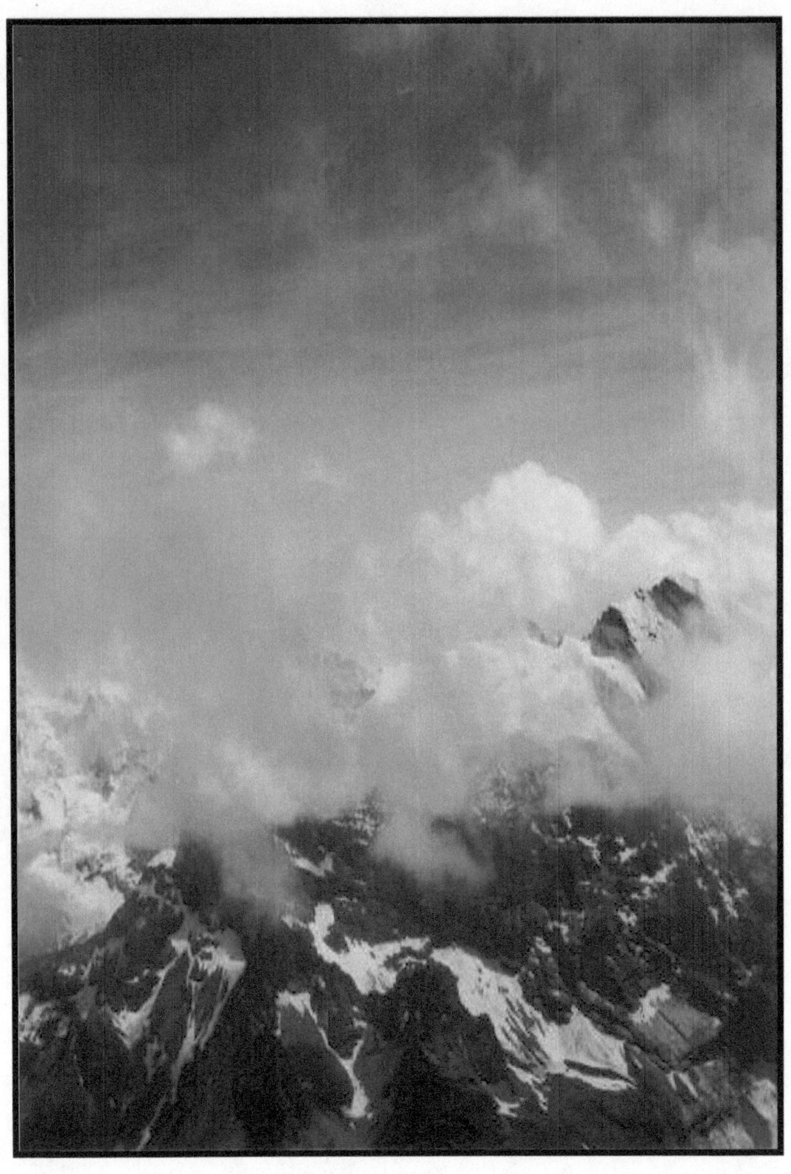

# water-bug rain

Semi-transparent skies
cloudy whys
how do we know----
they are really there?

Worth a thousand words
words---
not worth a tear
broken dreams
waterbug rain.

Worth---
the hiding
the reality
the movement of the bowels.

You'll never know----
the transparent whys---
each little raindrop---
every elusive roach---
as they scatter like
vampires against the light

Yet-----
Look to the skies---
the closing of eyes---
try to understand

What I can not reason
I must choose
choose
and believe in.

When the bitter colds of the season
Slap your face
Crack your lips
when the reaper whips through your heart aches

as if a blades of grass
forcing you to
look in the mirror
to see yourself
for what you really are
what you'll never be.

You must walk---
Your back to the wind
till the torrent subsides

Or

Cease to walk at all.

T. P. Prince

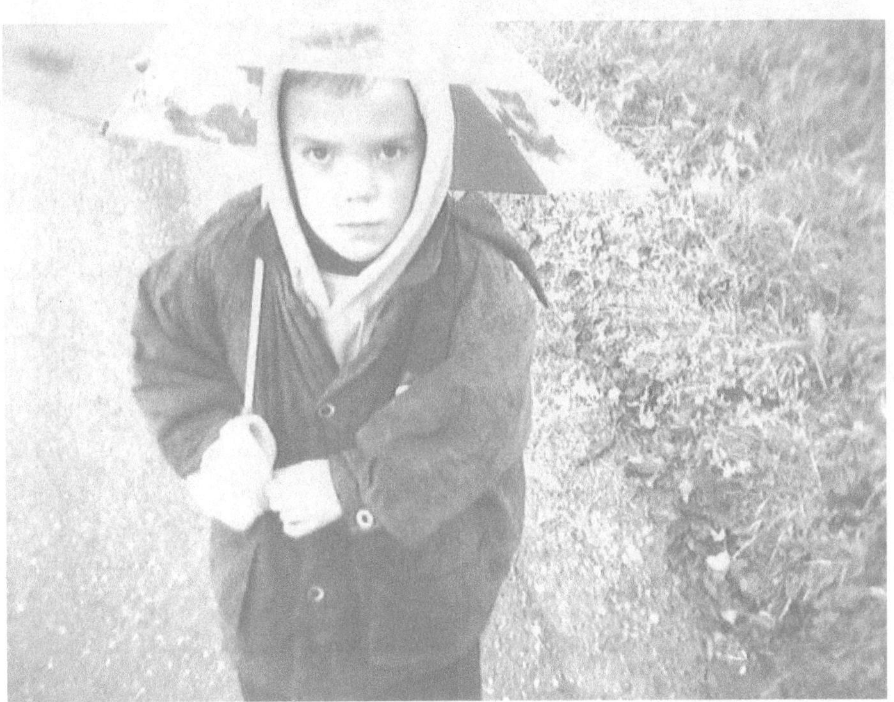

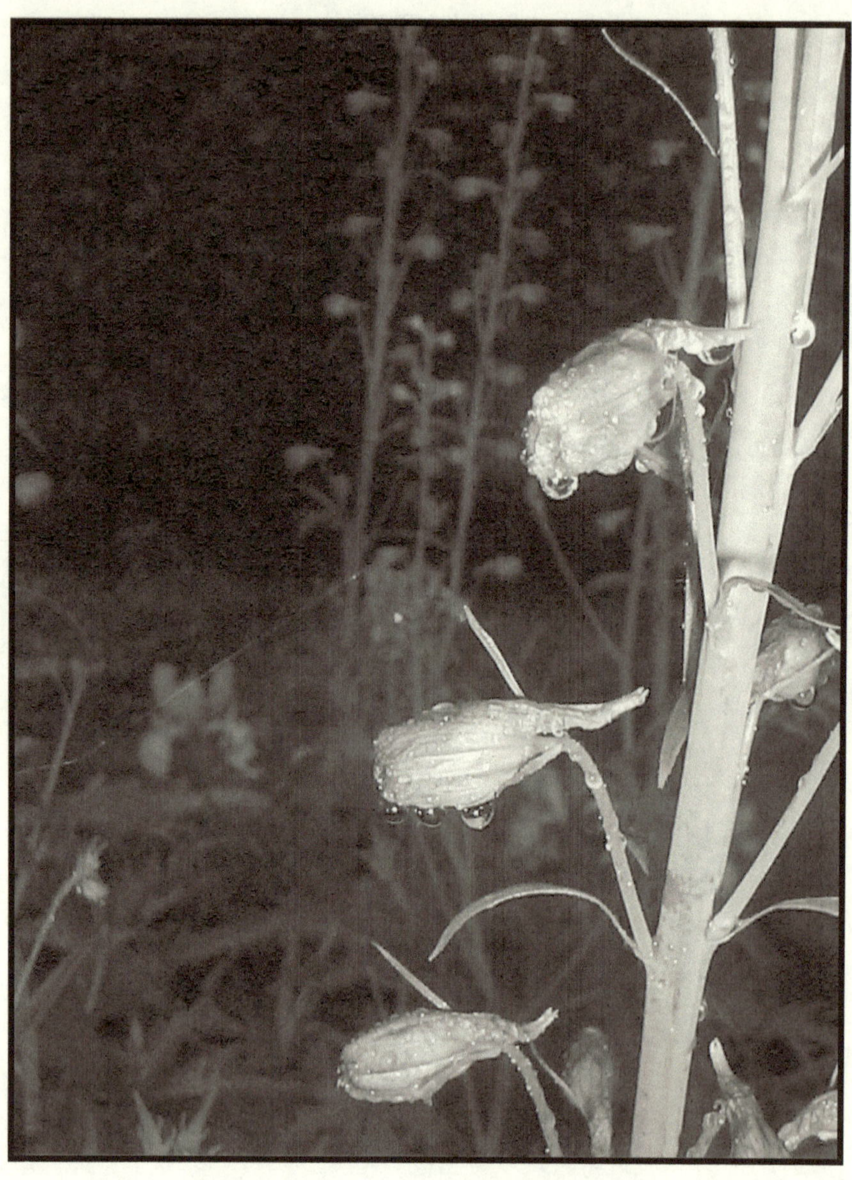

# Maybe Tomorrow

**For Debbie and Cynthia**

Why do you sulk,
little boy?
turning your back
to the crashing waves
the golden castles
bleached sand

do your tire at play?
or fear
they too
will go away---
why do your sulk…
little boy?

My feelings are burnt
trampled in dirt
and the waves
won't wash it away.

I long for the sun
(not the only one)
but it has been
eaten by
the Grey Dragon.

Will the waves ever
wash the sand away?

the sand -----it will stay
though the waves ev'ry day
so---little one
pick out a smile
to suit your own style
tempt the tempter---
the sea

in your own little way
as you laugh at your play
you gain victory over
the relentless sea

and then---
Tomorrow----
Yes---maybe tomorrow
The sun
will return
to stay.

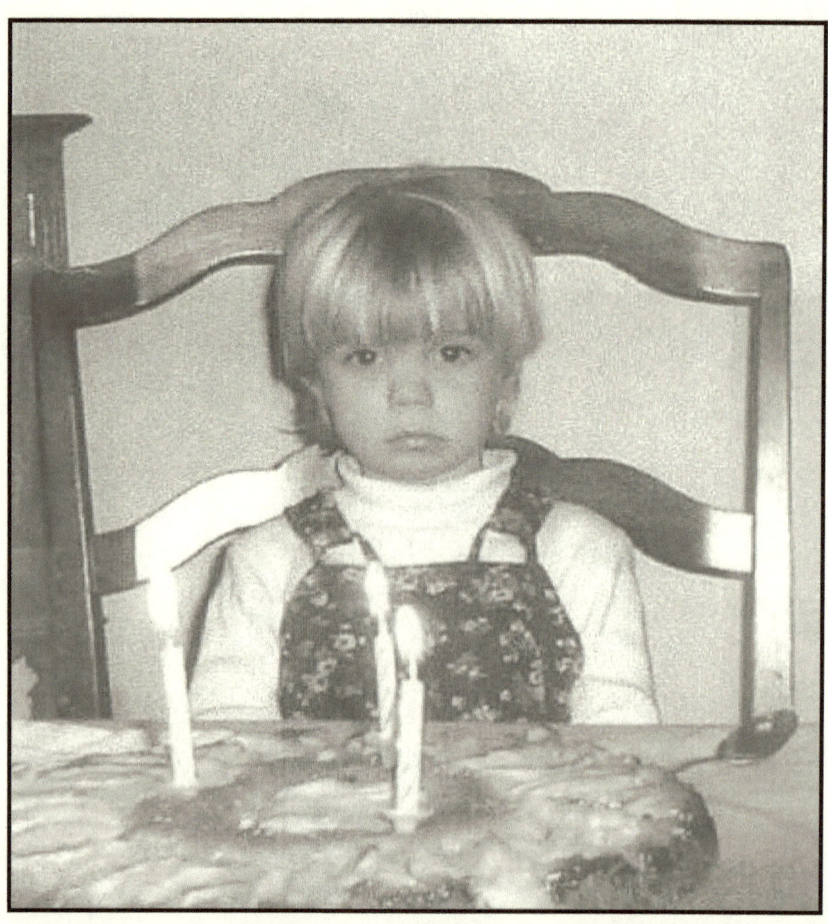

# spit not upon our eagled bird

**to Vietnam**

Freedom's land
Please beware---
too many people just
don't care
For the land in which theys live
selfish people with nothing
to give
nor any idea
how to live
Together----
in a world grown small.

Beauty breathless-
-colors bright
Please continue
to pursue
all the dreams
we had for you.

O fair people---
do not criticize
what you do not patronize
If you want your voices heard
spit not upon
our eagled bird.

Please good people open your eyes
first observe--
-and then surmise
this is not what was meant to be
in our nest of liberty.

Of our problems---
look around
curse not
our hallowed ground
but look inside
your person's own
You'll see why
the bird has flown.

God--- please help
our troubled land
extend to us
Your helping hand
Inspire us
before too late
help preserve
a nation great.

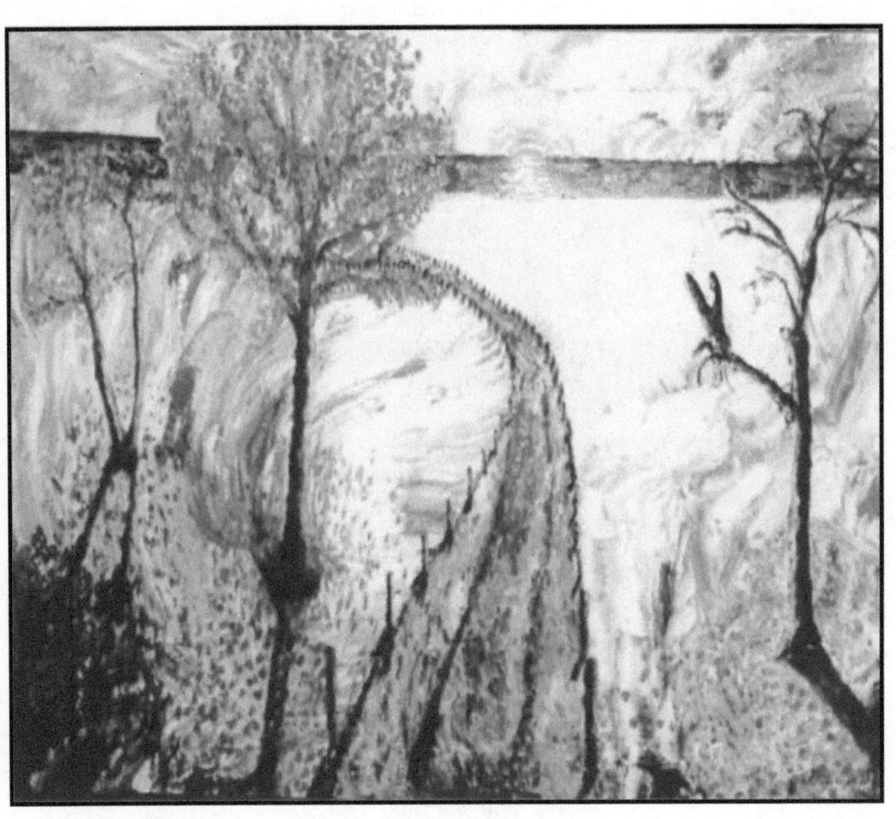

"the way back" tpprince 1990

# medley of meditation

Lingering lightening
discovers the night
a thundering raspsody
companioned by light
the basonic boom of a cloth covered kettle
blown through the sky
by a piping wind

a patterring rain
or
clear dripping Ginn
tap the rhythm of
the starry blues----

and I am alone---
I am---
alone
and I am alone
except for you.

Mountainous waves
wash glissening rocks
Star like gulls
stud a clouded sea
framing a floundering fiery cloud in the west
.
Salt and sand
fill mouth and ear
Salt and sand
constitute my tear
sunken footprints
design dampened sand---
Alone with the prints----
Myself ---
and the prints
Alone with the prints
that she ran.

The heated rays
of an awakening sun
Greet my body
to a new day come
My eyes open
quickly to close
to a blinding bright
that newly has rose.

A blarney breeze
coxed open my lids
to a beckoning light
I somehow forgot.

Love never leaves ----
Never leaves---
never leaves you

No---
Love
never leaves….
never leaves…
never leaves you
Alone.

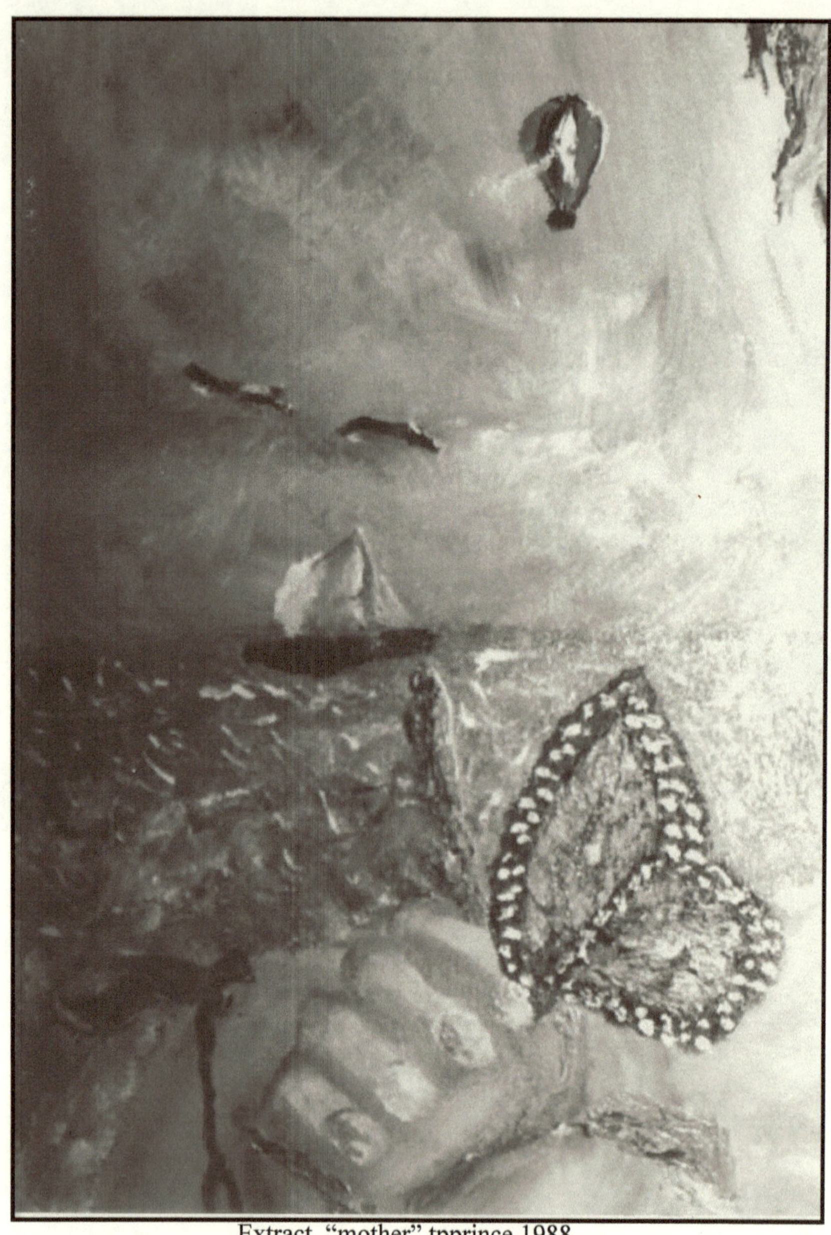

Extract "mother" tpprince 1988

# a candle without darkness

## to innocence

Out of darkness
emerged a light

Piercing the silence .
a stilletto ofsound

the womb of winter
sprouted springs
bunkers of cold
reluctantly began to thaw.

the flaming wax projectile
melted holes through the night
disguising darkness
in a robe of light

the candle waxed with care
fibered with
the slender whick of hope

a nearly inaudible sound
Challenged the silence
the quiet flicker of
the flame of love.

Trembling uneasily
it burned uneven tears in the darkness
love's voice
echoed off windless walls
unchallenged in the void

The light and sound formed a catchy day
and lured a curious sun
which lit
the minds of everyone

Bullets of light riddled the darkness
the noise of thought overthrew the quiet

the flame that lit the desolation?
no longer its enlightening glow

The gentle song of love?
could no longer be heard
mid self-bound minds.

What of the candle in such a light?

What is a candle without darkness?
is it to uselessly glow
illuminating nothing?

or does it…..

Disappear into eternity
into obscurity
into oblivion
into the cruellest place of all
an embittered heart.

T. P. Prince

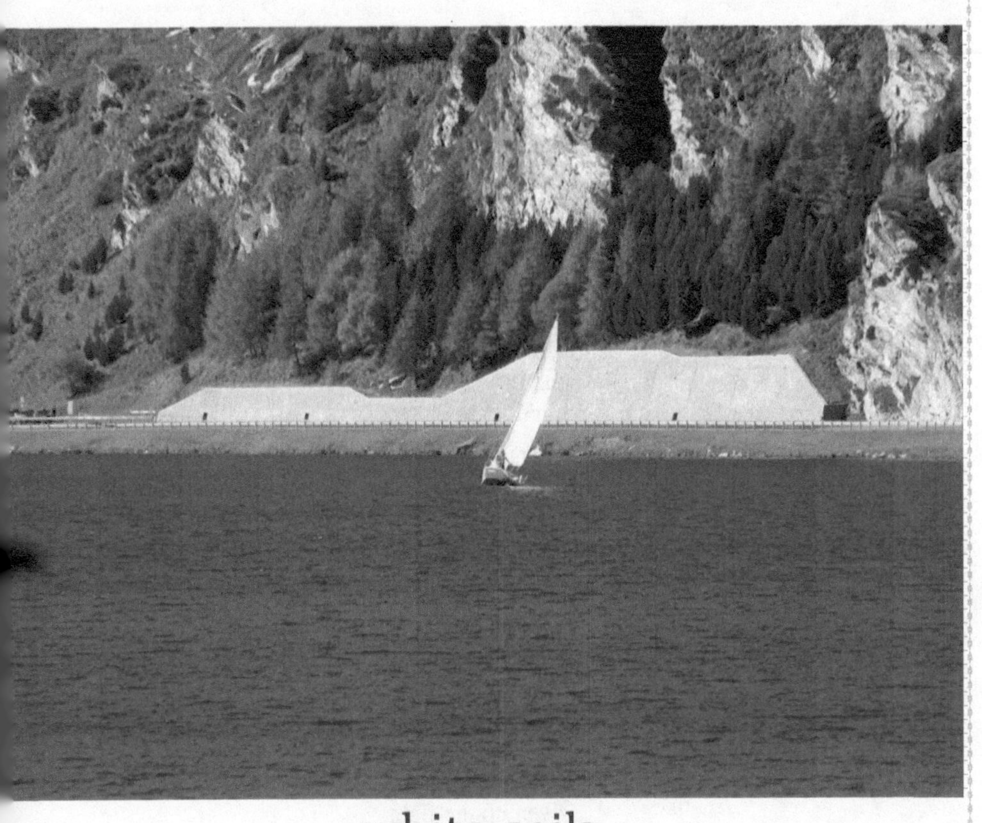

# white sails

*Ode to*
**Jason Engel**

April 29, 1981

Where hides justice----
when noble means
produce adulterous ends?
when courage
harvests lamentations
steadfastness stands
upon treacherous trap doors
that open no rewards

You have fought
the unfeatable foe
pursued the Knightly quest

sought the holy grail----
through the perpetual plains of doubt
over the mournful mountains of faith
across the fruitless valleys of hope
beyond the jagged jaws of despair.

_Your forged your way amoung
the forests of unrest
briefly rested
on the shadowy shores of victory
blindly gazed out
over the receding waters of life
set youir sail
across the uncharted seas of prayer

From a distance---
I could see your white sails
blown full by the winds of disire---
the desire for peace.

I first thought
it was the flag of surrender
that you had finally
given up the fight
Until I saw the force
with which it pulled at the mast
Pushing you across
those vast waters of torment
into the warm waiting arms
of the rising sun.

From the distance
I could no longer see---
your determined face
but that smile etched itself
forever
on my heart.

T. P. Prince

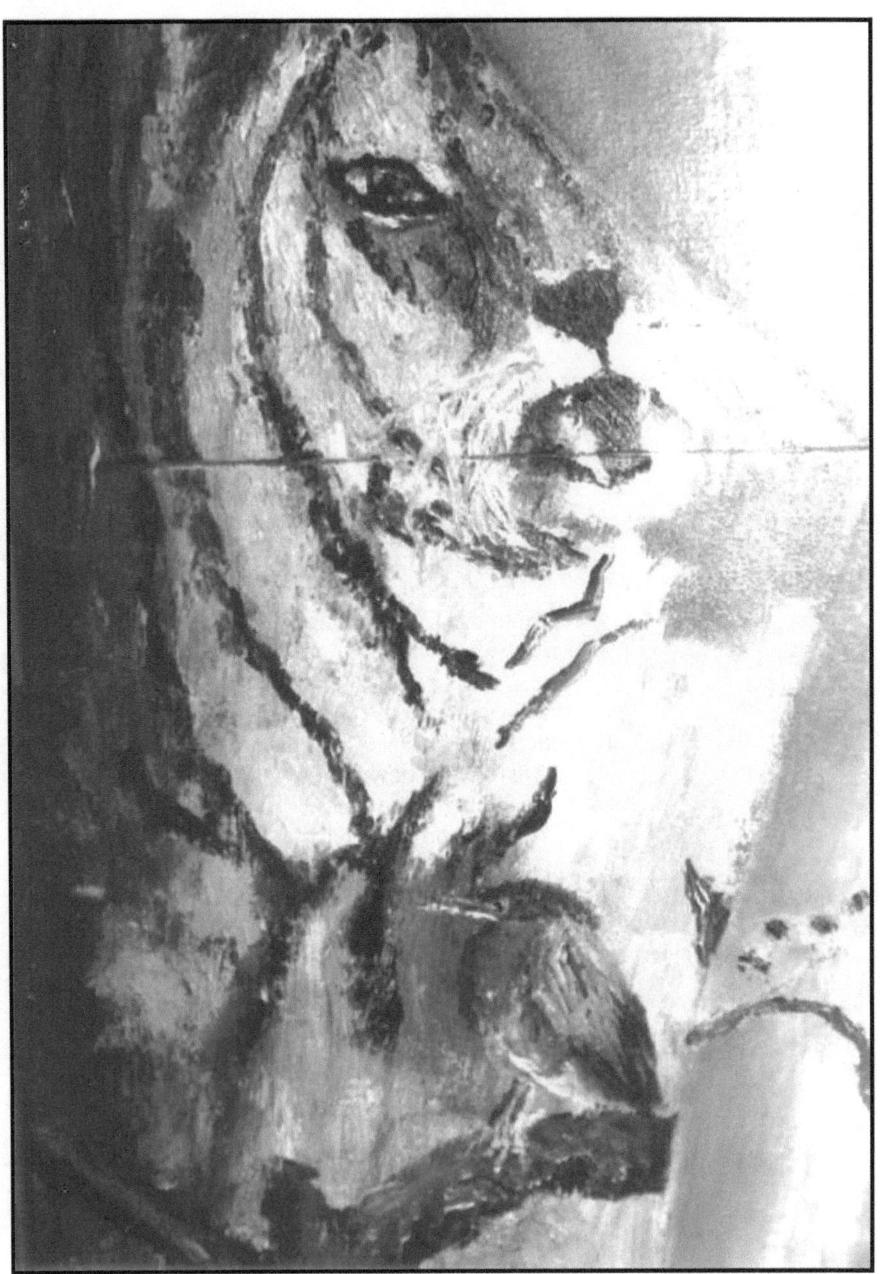

extract “mother” tpprince 1988

# The Wait

*For mom--Leslie Simmons*

People pass in melting smiles
little notice paid
to our empty open casket

Ones heart falters
falling like greasy hair
hanging in the face
spilling into eyes
joining lashes like webbed feet.

After awhile-----
we absorb the mishap with
a whispered profanity
return to the TV game show
and wait.

* * *

Hard hammered memories
Forgotten expressions of gratitude
Disfigured snowmen
dripping in the sun
faceless and forgotten
Demand the return of the Shah
and still-------
We wait.

Can't you feel it!
Taste it!
Drowned in it!
You must follow it
Chase it!
Catch it!
Lock it in your heart before-------

It Disappears

Why must we wait
our lives away?
* * *
We hate ourselves for-----
what's been forgotten
what was never known
what we waited too long to say---

till Eliot Sadness
gangbusts our convictions,
Till the ice-cubes dissolve
across more miles
lipless smiles---

Till the pain goes away
taking with it---
the only sign left
that love
still survives.

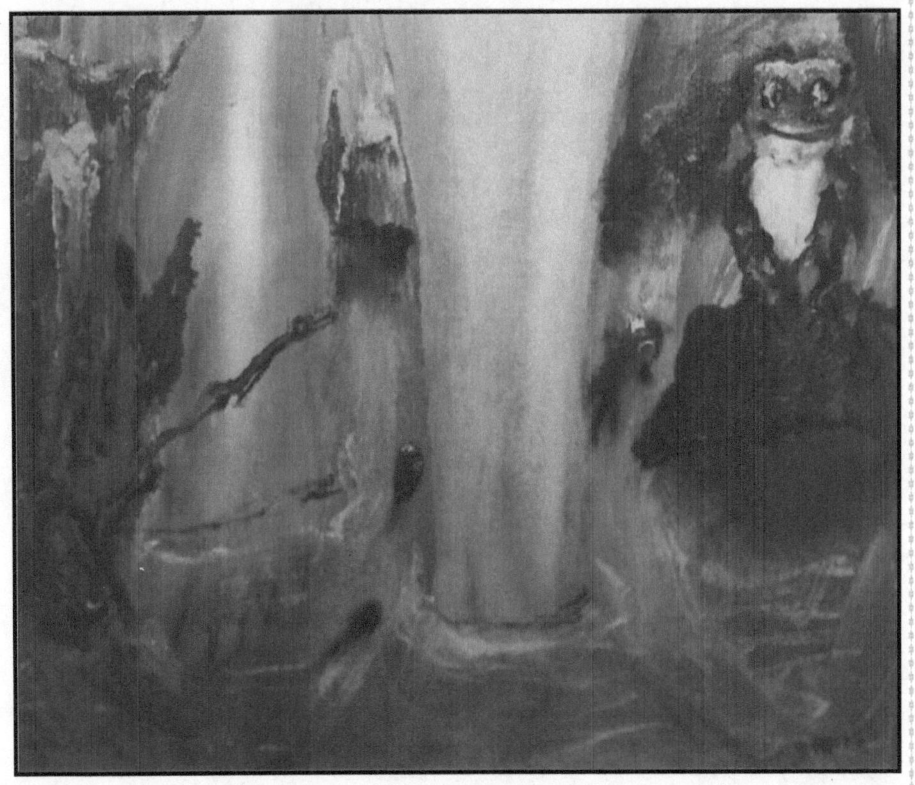

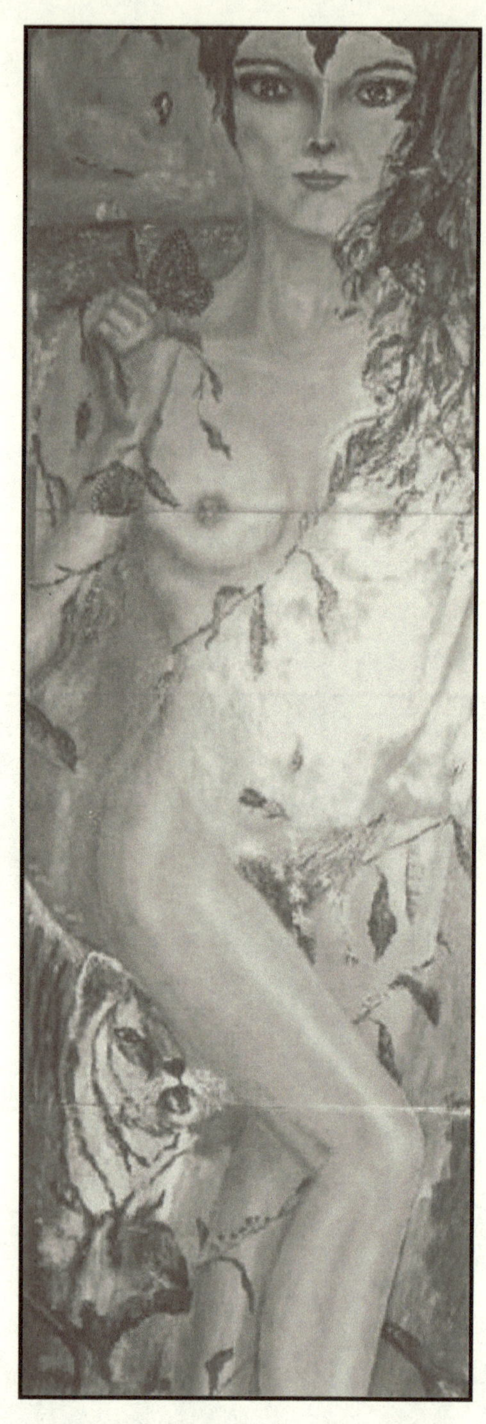

*« mother » tpprince 1988*

# Crests of Waves

for Killer

Again----
It seem------
to be raining

Again it is time-------------
for good-byes----
deep rooted sighs----
overcast skies.

It seems to me------------
I'm a bit in love
again-------------
---------you see.

A rather funny thing
You and me
We are the rain-------
sprinkling the white crested waves
of the morning sea.
We are the gentle showers------
washing leaves-----
nourishing flowers----
freshening life with beauty
refreshing beauty with life
Giving the world a fullness--------------
that makes me love it so-----
that I'll never-------
-----ever----
wish to let it go.

Does it seem to you--------------------------?
that even when the clouds are grey ---
the skies are blue?
that love----the little harpy
dances upon us
like raindrops on a summer puddle
making all things new

as we sit and reflect the skies
in the deep running waters
we call our eyes.

Again----------
as our love turns to grey-----------------
I stare out the window and remember
--------The sun
------warm touches
-----------dreams lost

Again------------
----it seems to be-----------
-------------raining
Again--------
--------------and again-
we say-------------------------Good-bye.

T. P. Prince

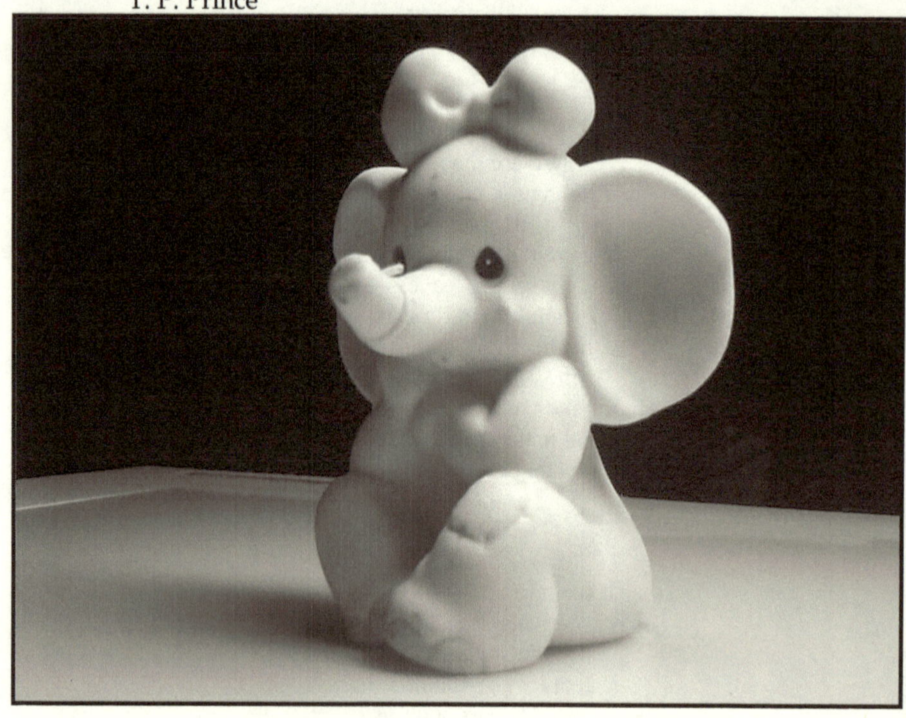

# two for all

## first love

Let our way be free
unhindered---------
by obligations
governed----------
by compassion ------------
not possession.
Look at me---------
as you wish I see you.
Think of love--------
as you would love-------- of you.
Drink my wine---------
as you would quench my thirst.
perhaps then----------
we shall be given------------ the sight
to see the radiance
that warms simple souls.

For if I am ----------but one
You--------- just alone
Uncommon factors
with no means of addition
We-------- will be
but a wasted baren hill
of sunless shadow.

But if I am------- you
and you------- are me
we may see in
not through each other
Life may yet ---------swim the sparkling sea

When the world--------- raises it sword
against the other
the blade must first
pass through the other.
When the sun warms one
the other shall not know cold

when the heart ache of one
------------places tears
on the cheek of the other.
the laughter of one
is heard through
the mouth of the other-------
that in ourselves
we are a combination of the two
that two is one
one is two
and two shall be
forever all.

T. P. Prince

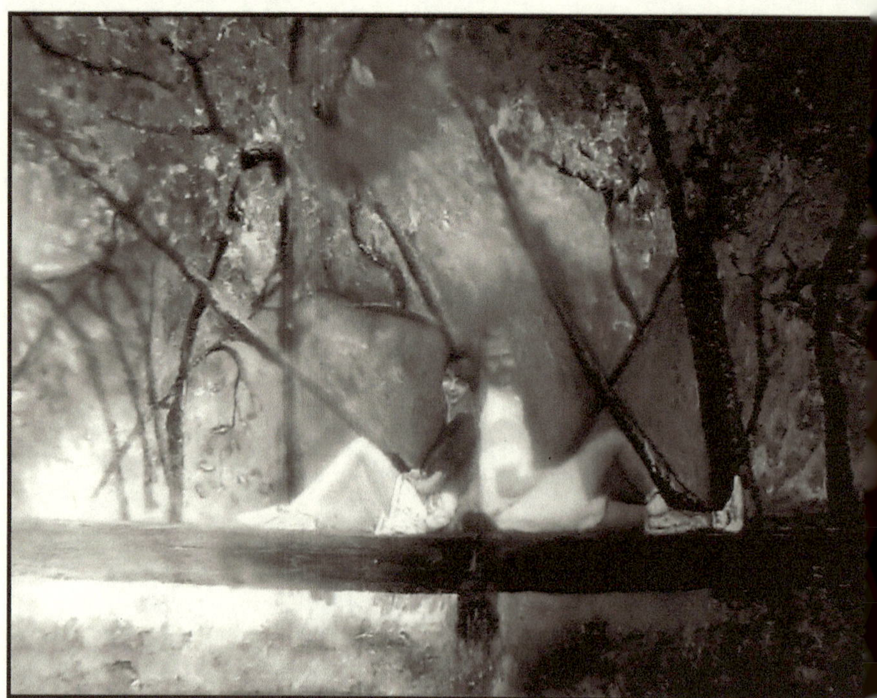

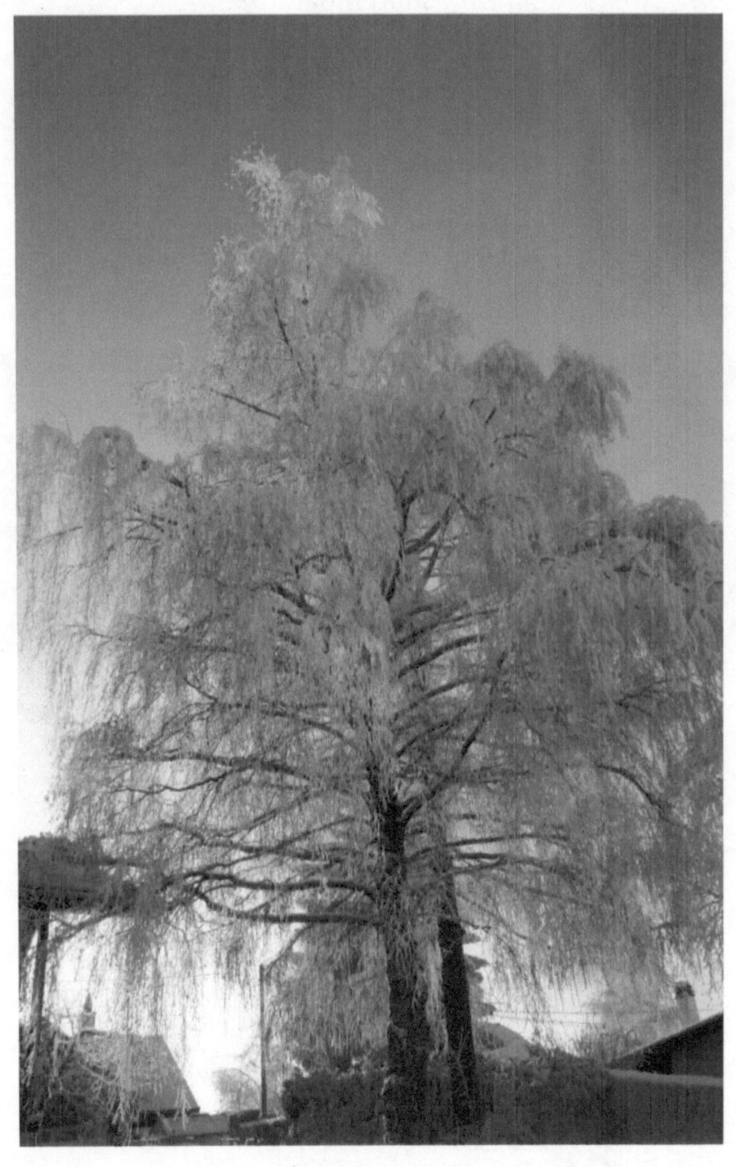

# Winter's Frost

## September 1993

The relevant Beauty of Existence---------
is Never perceived------
------------------Until----
The Searing of Summer Subsides -------

The brisk Whispers of Autumn
send their message through the trees----
If one strains ears
with the wisdom to Listen
the Muffled Message
Meanders among the Leaves

Life is -------
--Delicate----
Robust---------
-- Yet Fragile
it is not meant------------
---------to Last Forever.

We must-------
Proclaim it from
Lips in Song----
Cultivate it-----
with Living Deeds
Capture it----------
--------- in our Hearts-
Before----------
----The Starkness of Winter-----
Plucks them -------
-----from our Midst
Leaving us with -------
---------- marauding Memories
of the Beauty that left ---
its Fading Shadow
across our face.

Tenderly ------

-----Kiss the fleeting Children----
Openly------
------- Smile and Laugh with Friends…….
and strangers---
Tightly-------
---- Embrace your Loved Ones-----
For these are----
the only Seeds of Love-----
---------------That will grow again--
come Spring.

T. P. Prince

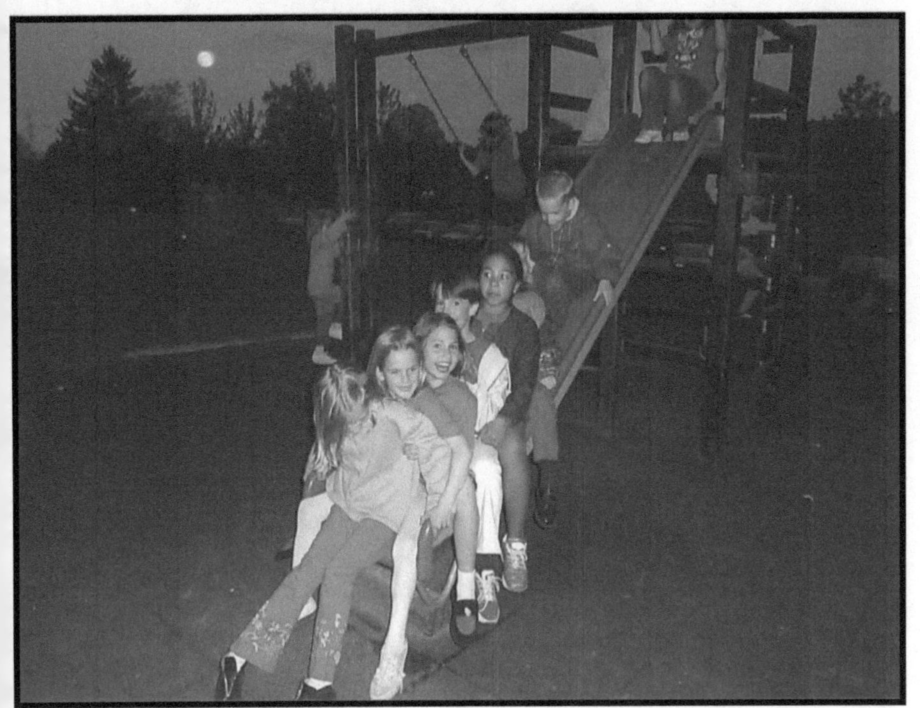

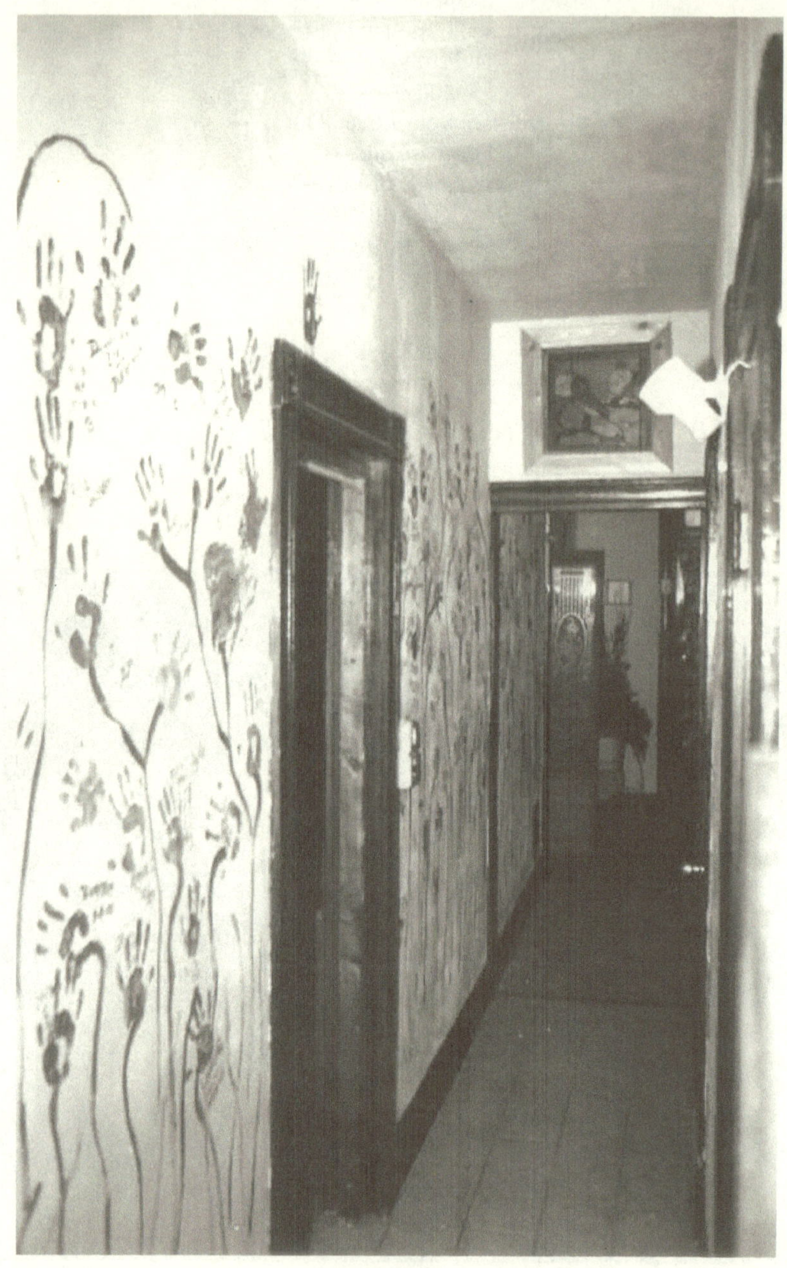

# Luxembourg

*Find our way*
*back------------*
*------------again*
*to the light*
*--------the warmth*
*Do the embers still*
*faintly glow*
*somewhere in the distant*
*corners of our hearts*
*in the furthest reaches*
*of our souls gone ascew?*

*The long nearly invisible*
*acclimatisation process*
*slowly turned our hearts--*
*----------our lungs*
*into huge hollow cavities*
*inefficiently taking up space*
*and more space*
*so we might survive*
*the descent into the Abyss*
*but we trade*
*our passion*
*lose our laughter*
*lose our sight ---*
*-------------- our touch*
*lose our compassion*
*-------------- our smiles*
*Lose all Hope.*

*Who is the enemy?*
*who will be the comrade?*
*who the saviour*
*who the destroyer.*
*who can love*
*who can not endure?*
*who can care*
*who can not despair?*

***who will understand***
***be they misunderstood***

***Can we find our way?***
***must we choose to stay***
***the way we are***
***caring less each day***
***acclimating ourselves***
***to the cold***
***the useless burdens***
***of mistrust***
***of covering one's ass***
***in case things go astray***
***bearing the souls of others***
***while locking our own***
***in a secret Luxembourg vault***
***with numbers and no names***
***to protect us from***

***anyone-----***
***Searching for the truth***
***-------for a path***
***--------for the way***
***to our hearts***
***------our minds***
***to our souls.***

***We can not find -------***
***----------------a direction***
***much less a path***
***We have trouble hearing------***
***the truth***
***We are always straining our ears***
***to try to pick up***
***the muffle of -----***
***---a lie***
***-----------of a failure***
***---------of a concession***
***-------------an imperfection---***
***Not from -----***
***-----------------ourselves***
***but from-----------***
***----------- the world around us.***

***We have acclimated ourselves***
***to lies***
***to callousness***
***to self-pity***
***to tears***
***to fears***
***to loneliness.***
***to counter positive productivity.***

***Our chests have expanded***
***our heads have ballooned***
***our hearts have hollowed***
***stretching to limits***
***to try to take advantage***
***of the faintest***
***breath***
***of true sharing.***
***That might still-------***
***be trapped in tiny bubbles***
***beneath the frozen tundra.***

T. P. Prince

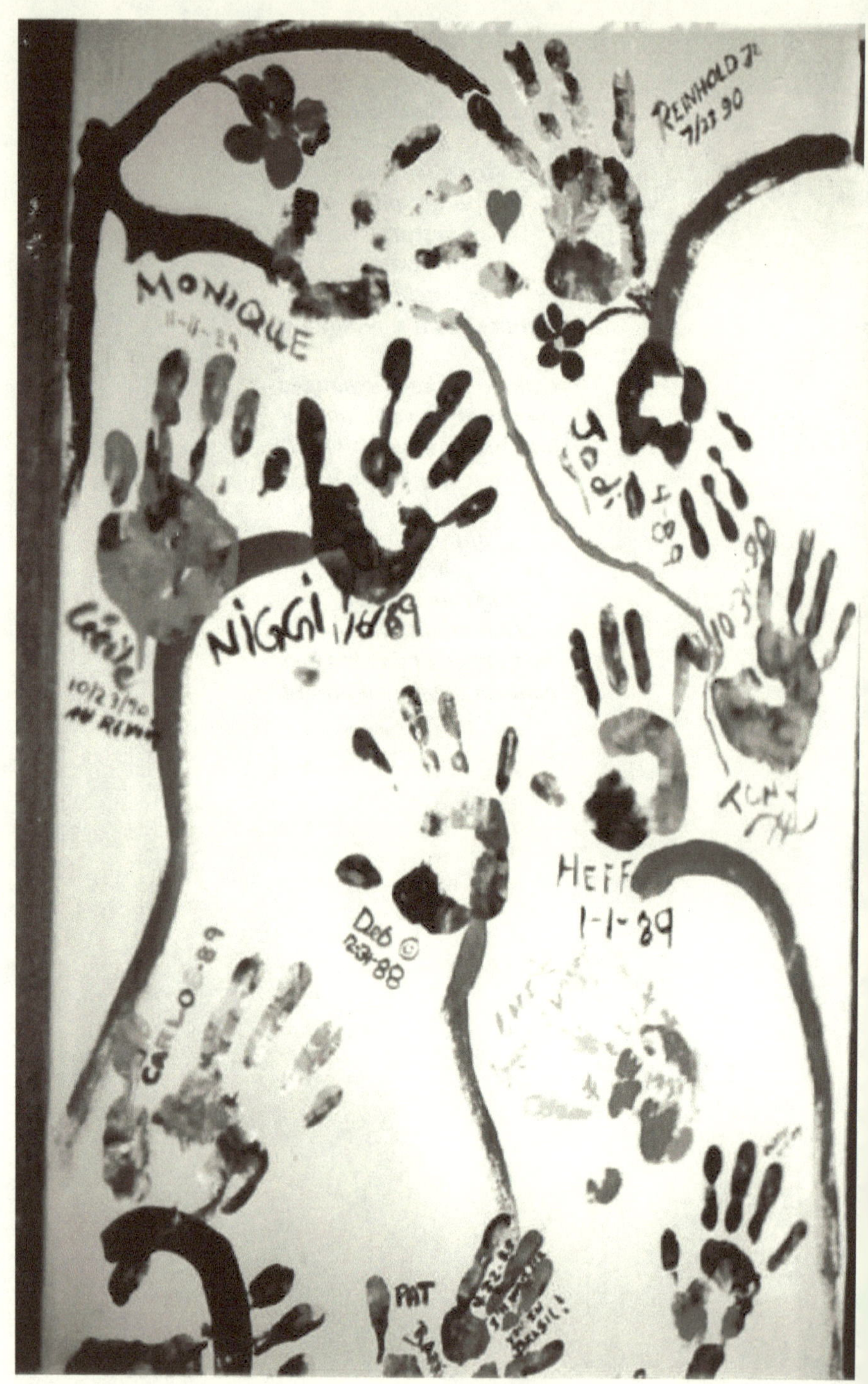
REINHOLD Jr
7/23 90
MONIQUE
NIGGI 1/1/89
HEFF
1-1-89
Deb ©
12-31-88
PAT

# SAM

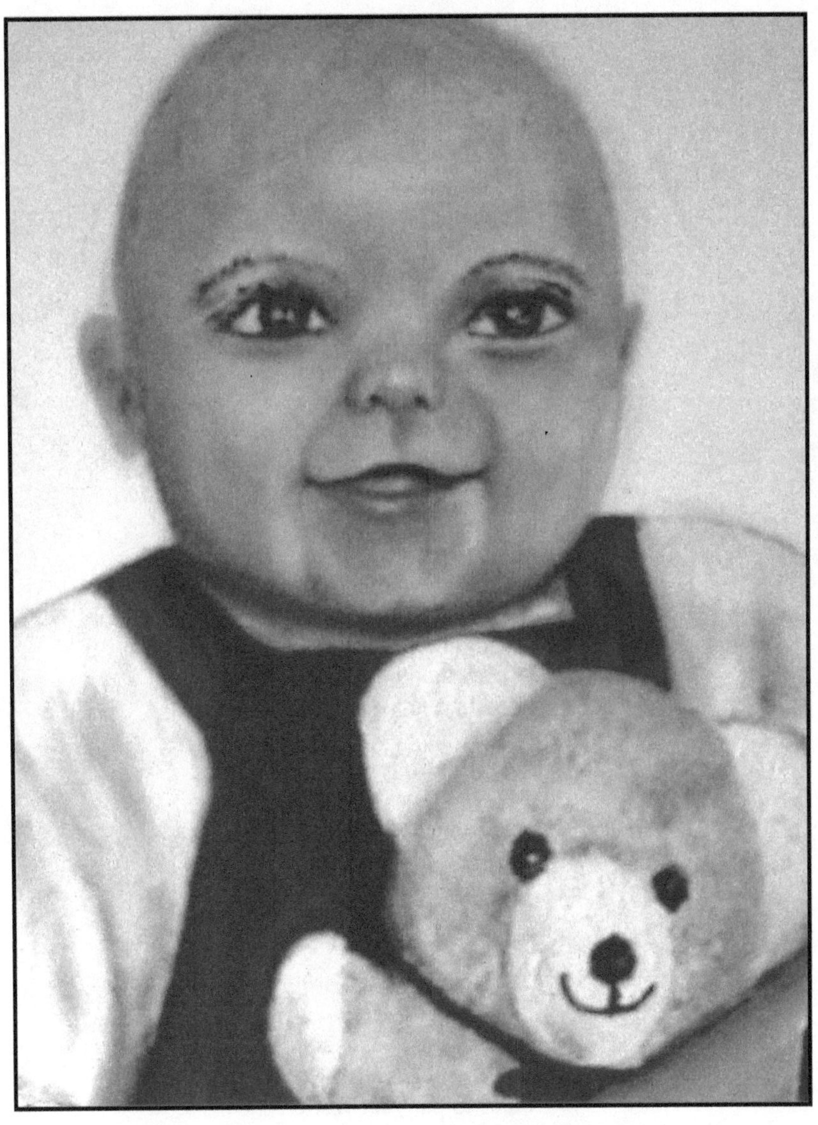

# Sam

## My buddy

mischievioius smiles
heart on spider legs
-willed to win
still waiting for confidence
Not yet kicked in.
you laugh as you learn
cry when you lose
sing in the car
dance when you choose
Pee in your bed
Snore when you snooze.
seriously playful
playfully intense
selfishly kind
a heart that's emense

you lie next to me
sleeping and dreaming
growing and knowing
Computing -----------
fears against wants
gains against loses
punishment against pleasure.
solidly delicate-----------
------------delicately strong
running ----------
---then hiding
please tell me-----------
-------what's wrong

You're as clever as the problem
a cunning little clown
quick as a conclusion
expressive as a frown
Place to put your world

Space to store the future
You organise corners just for you
a corner for me
a corner for hope
one left for dreams

You are like me
but you are better

Afraid to fail
scared not to try
terrified to give up
hesitant to reply
with answers you know
might make others cry

the summer .......clouds
color ------------the retreating
------------------of my sun
I wonder ------------about God
the sky -----------the moon
myself------
--- and my son
he makes me ----------laugh
makes me ---------cry
he helps me --------------to love
to dance ---------- to sing
he is not the answer------
---- he is the prayer

The illusive Reason
The undeserved Reward
The haunting reflection
The badly needed Direction
to a life suspended
in Doubts

# Sandy Beanhead

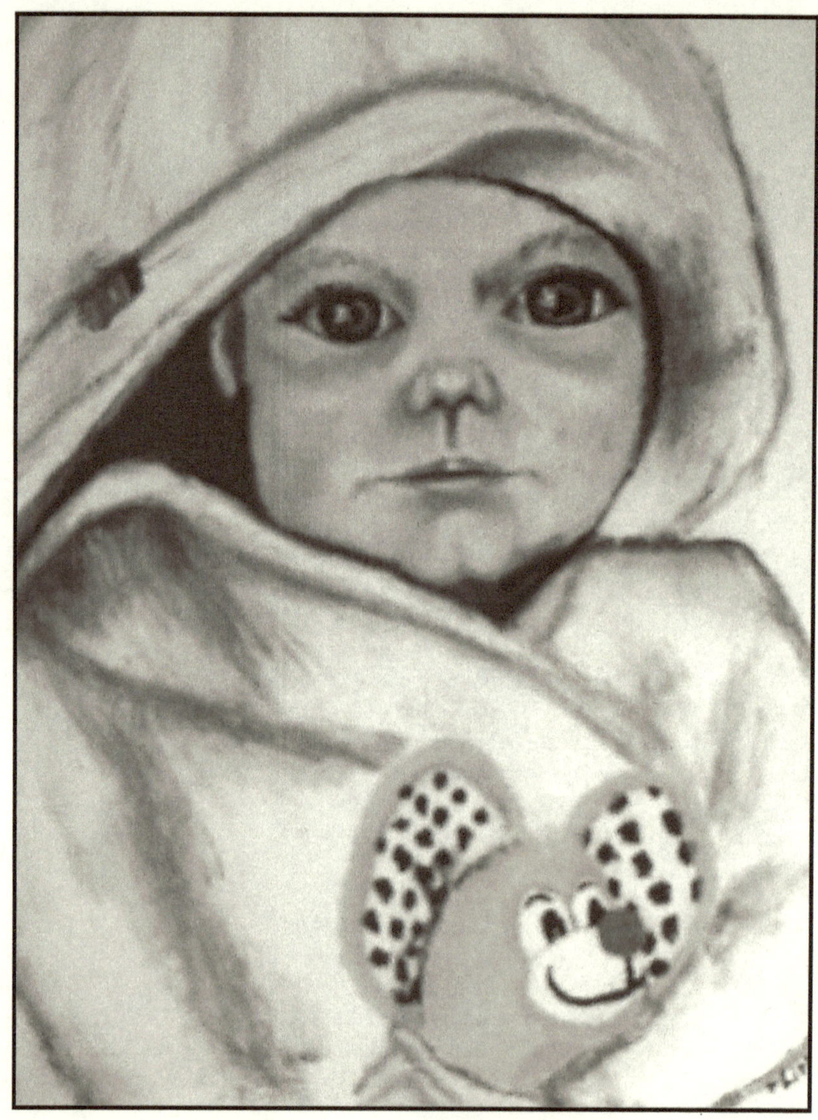

# Sandy

## Sandrine my little Beanhead princess

Delicately complicated by uncertainty
beautifully enriched with frivolous intensities
best expressed after darkness hides the sharp lines
she is too much like me
too alert when night falls
too sleepy when day breaks the fall
lost in the dreamworld
that brings allumination and warmth
to the cloaked evening
but adds nothing
to the reality of the bare naked day.

like myself -----
when I was young
the perfect balance -----
--------of imbalances
her head in a ficticious book
her mind in the cloudy altituteds.

she has often saved me------------
--------from myself
----------from my discontent,
---------my unacknowledged ignorance
-----------my self destructive lack of faith
she smiles --------
--------that unbalanced tetering smile
she askes ---------
---------that perfect question
when I am lost in myself ----
-------and finds me------
------------------again.

I would not of made it here-
------------without her
She has rescued----------

---------------------- my innocents
paid the ransom
to keep my heart from------------
------------------ total destruction
I can feel her compassion
when she hears a story----
-----reads a book
I can see -----------
--------the tear in her eye
the teares already in her heart
when the tale is sad--------troubled
I can see--------
the glow in her soul
the gleam in her eye and spirit
when the happy endings arrive
the evil is laid to rest.

I see in you-------------------------
the courage--------
of Joan of Arc
the beauty------------
of the Snow Princess
the spirit-----------
of Jessica in King Kong
the unshakable vision------------
of Cinderella
the wholesomeness-------------
of Sandy Beanhead.

I hope---------
I have not poisoned you
with all the fairytales
for you are the only real fairytale
A dream come to life.

see your confidence growing ------------
-----------your spirit rising
your potentials----------
gathering interest in the bank
the joys---------
of your achievements
the frustrations-----------
of your failures

I watch as you gain momentum
-------tears fill my eyes
-------helium fills my heart
contentment sieges--
------ my imprisoned soul
forcing me to acknowledge------
--------- that I chosen
the path of least regret.

# Little Beanhead

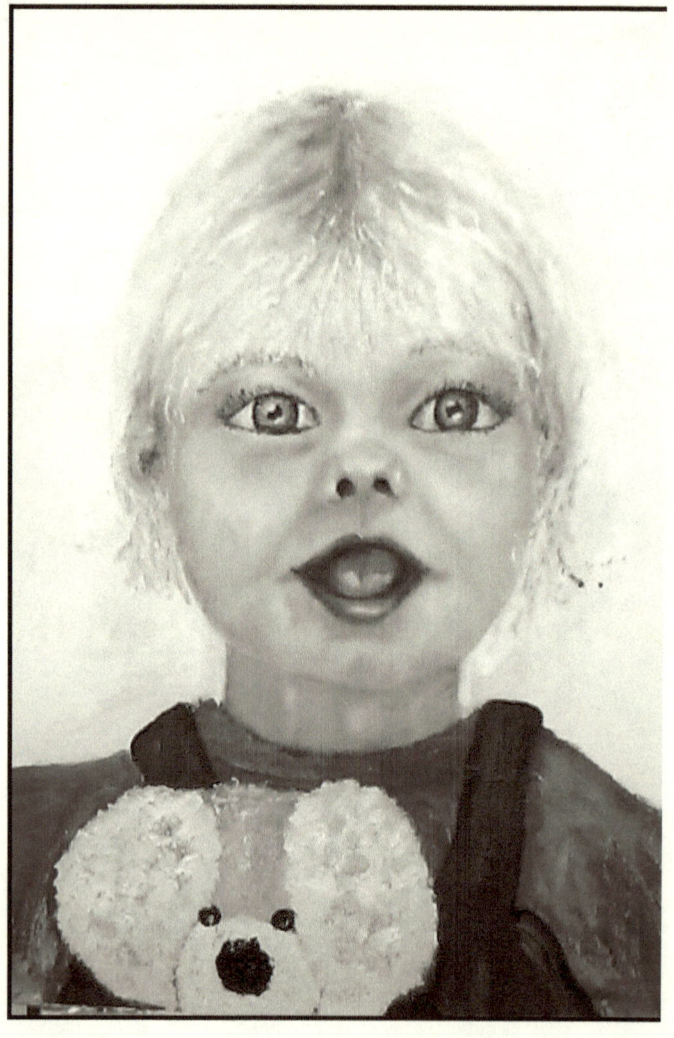

# Little Beanhead

## Stephanie- my spirit set free

I can not picture you----
can not vision you
can not image you
without the endearing smile
that total body laugh
that captivating impish grin

You have completed the trilogy
---------filled in
the remaining holes----------
in my being
set the legend in motion.
You have the character
----------------- the resolve
----------------the desire
--------------the need
to make it all happen

Blond, Blue strong ------
---------------- demanding -
Playfully interested----------------- in everything
from toilet paper surface tension
to feline dentistry
you never stop seeing-------------
----------------------things that I have forgotten
------------things that I missed
-------------------------things that I never
--------------------------- knew existed

You have tested my knowledge
my patience
my intelligence
my moral strength
I have mostly-------------------
------------------- failed miserably
but you only laugh
and tell me-----------------

------------- keep trying
some day-------------
I will get it right.

You lay your head--------
-------- on my shoulder -
You run to me -------
------when I get home
You call me-------
------ when you fall
You give me pieces-------------
-----------------of your cookies
------------------your flowers
---------------your heart

Fiercely independent
helplessly sociable
you bother ---------
your brother to tears
when he tries plays
but refuse to share
your games with him
even though-------------
you love him so very much

is the first name -
you choose to speak
"here Sam-------------.here Sam"
when you finally do give him back his toys.
He will not be mean to you
he will not take them from you
he will not hit you back.

It is hard to be so jealous
and
to love you so much.
this will be a problem
for the many people
who will love you

you are---------- the blanket baby
the others have-------
-------------- a dog

-----------------a teddy

You are the hardest one
----------------to understand
---------to teach
---------to direct
but---------------the easiest--------
to love.

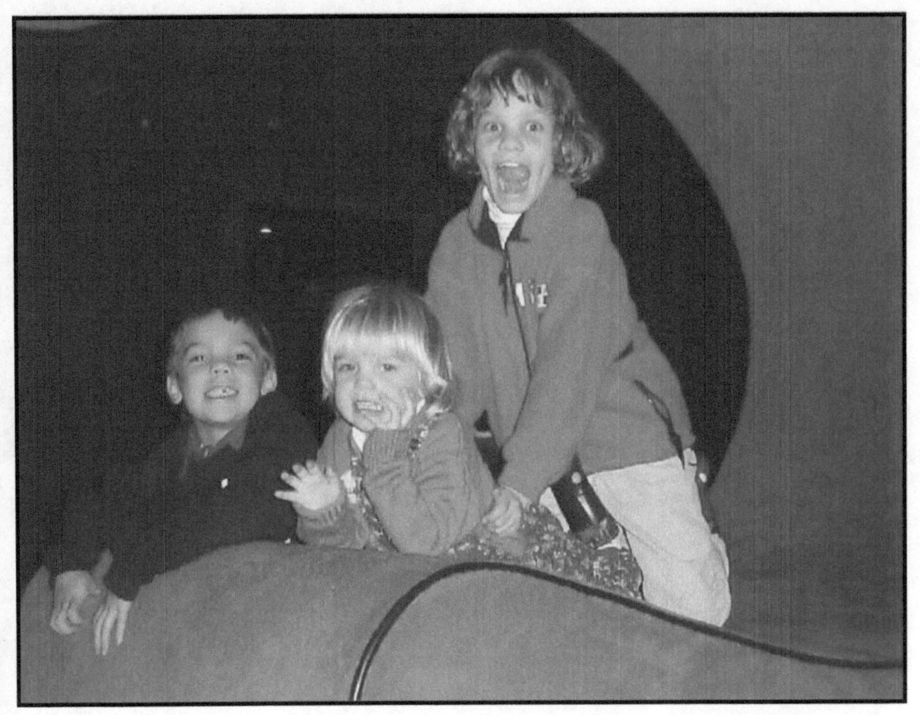

# Secret

smiles that illuminate a heart
like a match lighting a candle
a childs sloppy hug
warm,unrestrained and clear as
spring ice melting from a puddle
a single misformed word
springing from a emerging mouth
dada---mama---up--up
please hold me
please touch me
please love me
dada---mama---up--up
the arms reach up
to a knee---to a hip---to a height
arms around a neck
sloppy secretions run down a milky mouth
continuing down another face and neck
smelling of day old milk and urine
they refuse to let you go
refuse to return to the land
of feet and head high obstacles
that block their way
bumping heads when they try to rise up
falling from chairs when they get curious
to see the things that
exist in the land above heads
dada---mama---up---up!

Get down now!
Leave me alone for a minute!
Can't I get a moments peace!
Can't you see I'm busy?
I love you but not now please!!
You're driving me crazy!
not now---
not now please---

not now!

The cycle begins----
the secret is lost.
The child hesitates
the moment is lost
the child turns away
she washes her face
he hugs his teddy
he begins to suck his thumb.

The man silently watches
the television-
the street through the window
his wife behind the magazine
she watches him watch
she watches herself
filling in the blanks
with bright colors
without answers

The glass could be broken
with a word
with the secret word
but she is afraid of-------
the wrong reply
the wrong interpretation
the truth
and the consequences

The darkness begins to fall
the man looks to his wife again
He thinks of the potential
fall-out should he speak
should he touch
should he reach up?
dada---mama---up-------
-up----
-------please!

T. P. Prince

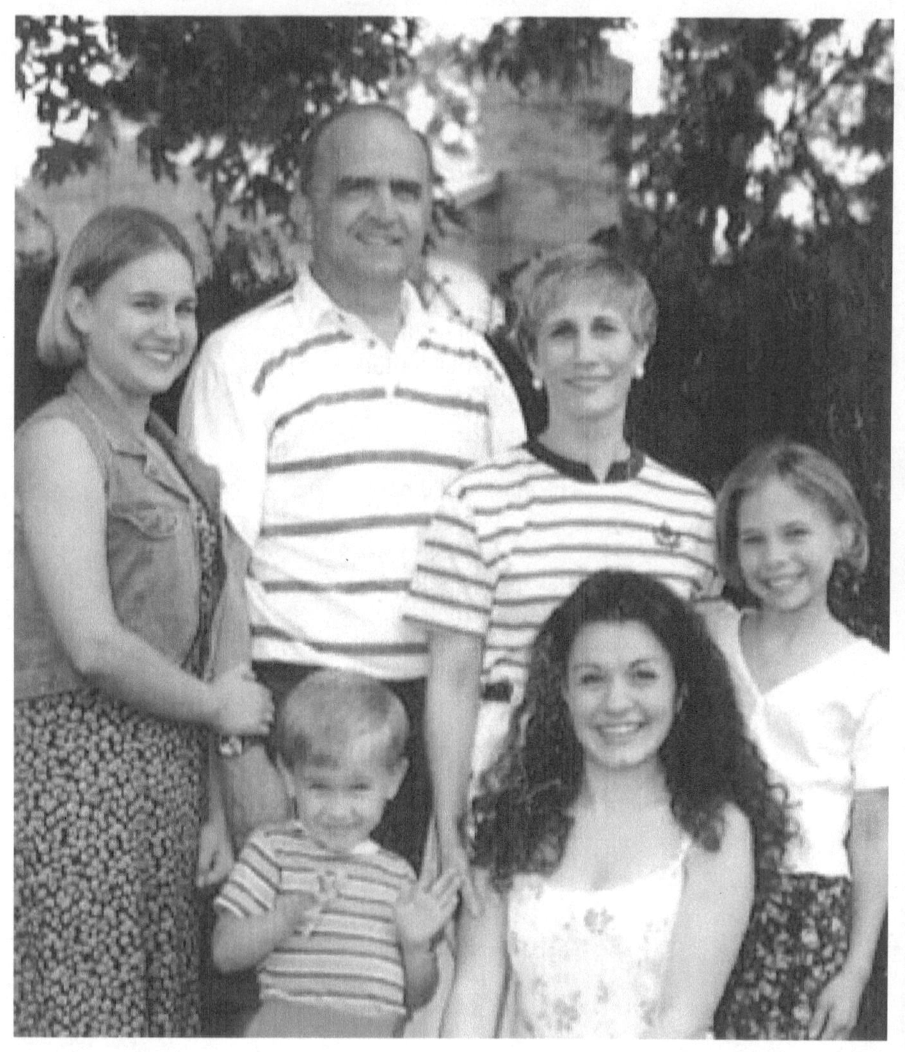

# Husband father hero

*Ray*

I watched him---------
find ---------------
-----------a smile
-------------a laugh
-------------a life.
effortlessly------------
full of-----------
-------care
-----sincere enthusiasm.

I watched him---------
----------------marry
--birth and baptize
------raise, praise
love--------
--a family
-a church
-a community
----a life
--a God

I watched him-------------
try----------
to teach his son-------
----------to ride the bike
his daughter-----------
---------drive a car
His wife---------
-----------to understand
his family--------
---------to belive

I watched him--------
laugh--------
---------at stupid movies
--------at dumb jokes
------at children at play

---------at family squables
------at a silly world
-----------at his foolish self
Full of--------
----------compassion
-----------desire
----------the spirit
of youth--------
of nature--------
-----------of Christ.

I watched his world------------
when it found out---------
he had taken his leave.

I watched them------------
-----------sigh
-----why?
---kiss
-cry.

He had touched-----------
-------------so many
-------------in so many ways.
He still touches us---------
with ----what he has left
----what he has done
---what he will do

He watches me-------
as I dance---------
----with my children
Sing-----------------
-----with my son
Cry---
--with my sisters
Laugh----
-------with my brothers
Help----------------
-------a friend
remember--
----the dead.

He watches us------------
run---------------
------to a ball game
listen---
----to the music
Laugh----
--------------at a movie
share-----------------
---------a joke
ride--------
----our bikes on the streets.

He knows-------
that we------------
-------------love him
-----------miss him
We know-------------
that he----------
----------loves us
--------------misses us
By the things---------
-that he did
by the things
----he left behind

He will know
--our love
By the things-----
-----------we do
by the things---
-----------we leave behind.

T.P. Prince

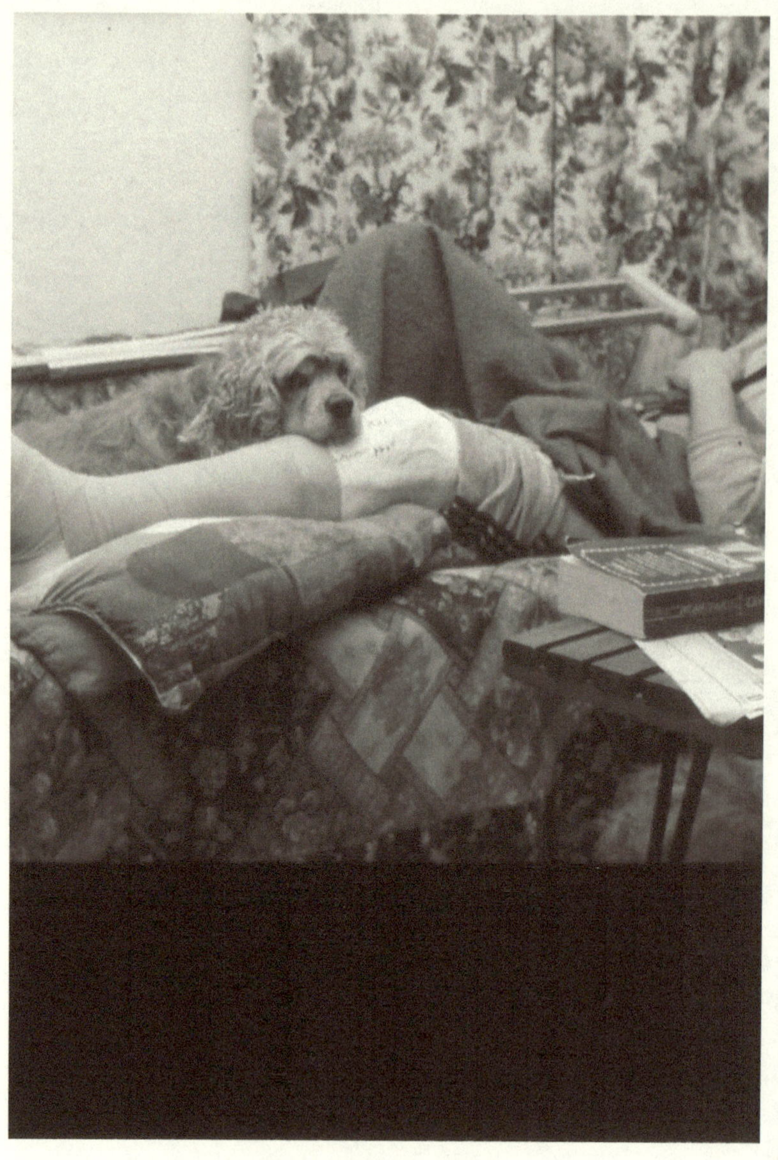

# *Shipwrecked*

**For my little Rose**

I never say enough-------
-------- show enough
--------display enough
-------help enough
-------support enough
I don't know------- why
---------nor when
-------if ever
it will get better

You have-------- worked
-------tried
---------retried
sufferred----------- the loss
hoped --------for the best
loved--------
as best you could

One must love----------- themselves
before they can love------
---------anyone
---------anything
--------else
I no longer--------- love myself
This --------scares me
------------depresses me
---------drains
my inner being
till -----------I fear
I may dry up ------
------ blow away.

This is --------new
------------foreign
to me.
I don't know---------
how ---------to handle it
-----------combat it
---------rid myself of

--------the gnawing discontent

I blame---------- everything
but----------
the only real culprit-----------
Myself.

I have ----------lost my faith
-------------lost my smile
-------------my self reliance
I flounder--------- in the mist
not knowing--------
if I am going---------- forward
-----------------backwards
----------------up or down.
I am floating-----------
in the dead calm
--------- a waveless sea.
I cling to three buoys----------
SVS-------- SJS-------SCS
to keep myself floating
as I wait for -----------
---------- breezes
-------------direction
----------- courage.
I fear --------
that I am keeping them------
from floating freely--------
----- toward their destinations
that I am keeping you---------
----------wedged
in this stagnant either
of motionless quag

I try ------
-------to shout orders
from my sinking captains chair
but can not-----------
------------make up my mind
---------which direction
-----------which sail to raise
-------which way to push
on the till

to get us out of the mire.

It is too nice a place---
----- to leave
but--------- too empty a place
------------to put my heart
at rest.
it is too safe a place---------
---------to depart
without a reason---------
-----------to push you away
-------------a dream
to pull you toward.

I can not ---------ascend
I refuse--------- to pull back
My heart-------- my spirit
-----------is being used up
---------eaten up
by the contented cow
which gives---------
----------everything
---------nothing.
each day I grow----
----- smaller
-------weaker
-------more complacent
-----------more critical
And I don't really seem--------
--------to care
that is the scariest part
--------of all
once we begin-------
--------to cease to care
we begin------
---- our descent
---------down the crater
of the faithless
---------into the jaws
of in-humanity

I still---------
hang on to-------

the floating raft
of hope
clinging to---------
--------its slippery deck
I will not leave-------
I will not let go-------
memories ---------comfort me
kind thoughts-----------
give me strength
your love----------
-----------keeps my faith
-----------alive.

T. P. Prince

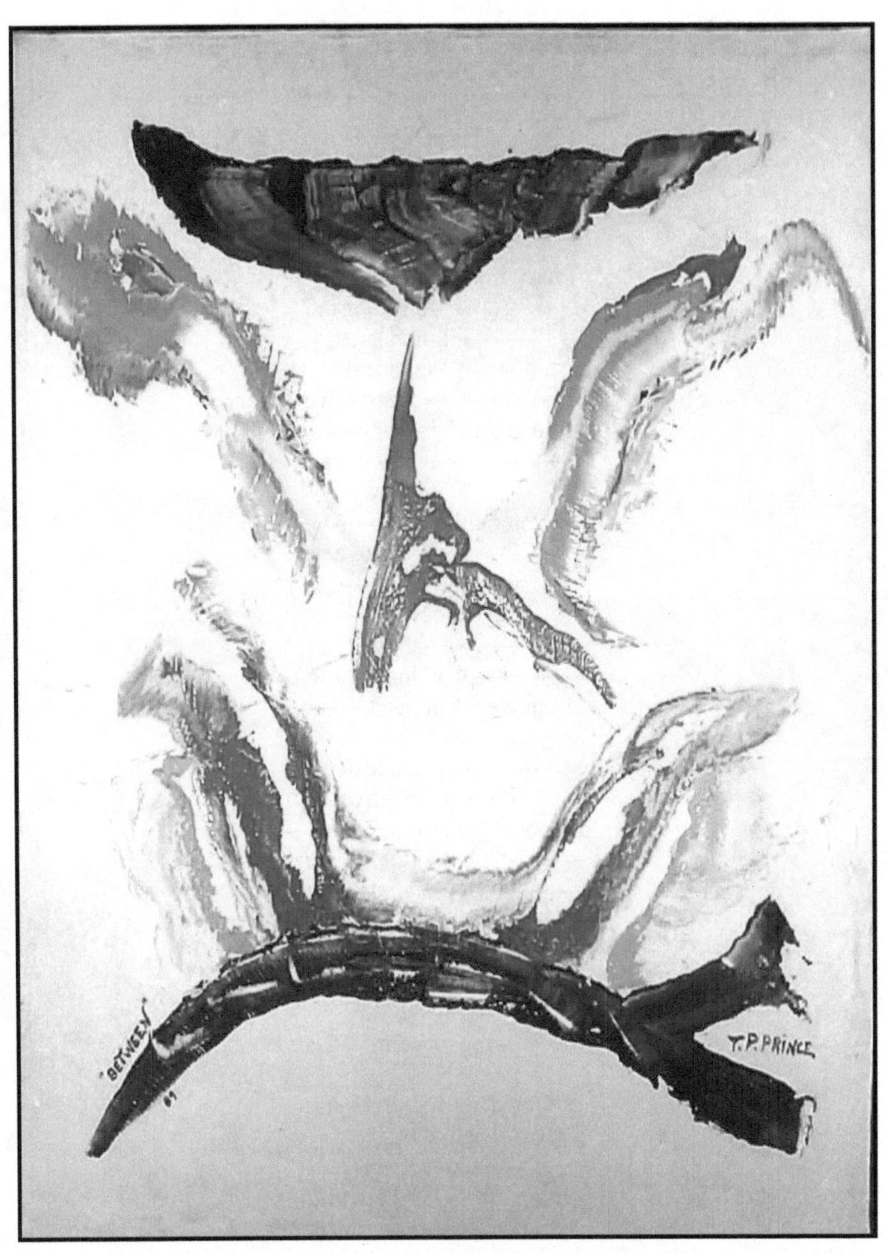


*« between » tpprince 1989 oil 40 by 60*

# Switch or Land

Hard to feel-----------
difficult to know------------
from the outside
I have not found her---------
------------to be warm,
---------light hearted
-----------supportive
--------------- instructive
She grows her own---------
------------her own way

Her children--------
--------------------- love her
though-----------
they seldom-------
-----------show it
---------------just don't know how
one does not need-------
---- to be
-----------competitive
-------- combative
but one must still be------------
----------- individually tough
----------------silently strong
---------------quietly optimistic
---------------unrelentlessly striving
to find-------
----------- the way,
------------the place in the circle.

I have not found it here
I belive ------
------I never shall
I am not-------- her child
I am not --------her protegee
I will be---------
---- lost here
she will ----------

------consume me
as feed for her own
She will take in all
but she must-----------
----------- in the end
favor her own

She is not differrent from-----------
any other mother
but like all children
mother will always be---------
------- the best
------- the most perfect.
They will see faults---------
--------- disappointments
------------holocosts,
------------- banks,
---------- mislaid trusts
but
she has----------
---------- a kind voice
she has -----------
-----------a lovely face
that smiles and shines
she will-----------
----------- take care of her children
they will----------
---------- take care of her.
together they will---------------
----------- feel safe
------------ will be content
but they will also---------
be short of----------
-------------vision.
Short of-----------
-----------------disappointment

T. P. Prince

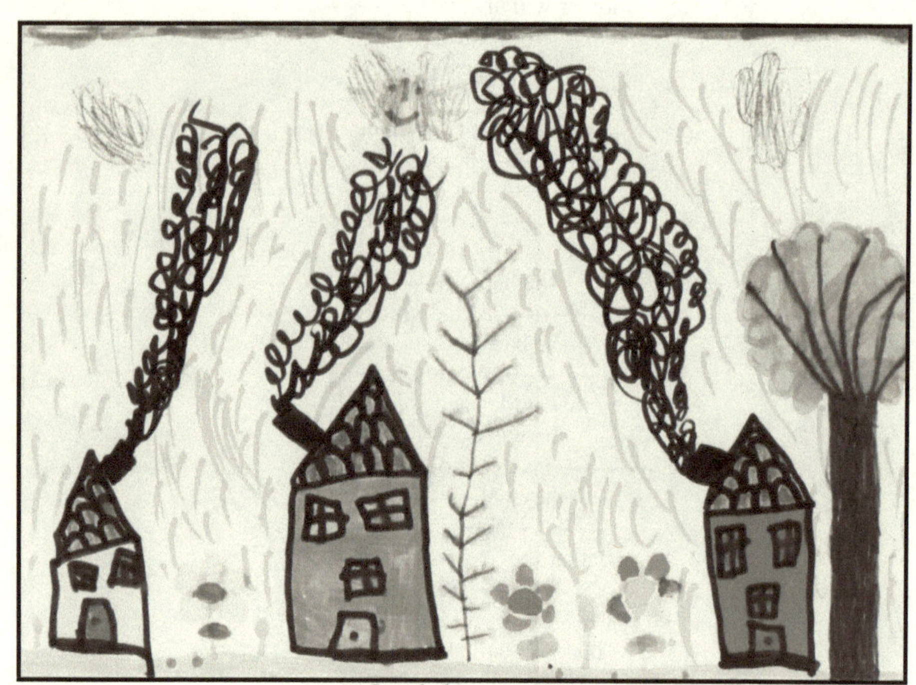

Sam's houses 2000

# why two kay

Milleniums------------------ change
People scour the heavens ---------
for a sign------------
---------------in the mud of the floods
-------------in the fallen trees of the storm
--------------------in the computer hysteria
of a generation
------------------in the frivolous counting
of passsing time
Hoping to find-------
------ meaning,
------------- faith
------------ reason
in existence---------------
-----------------the existence of humanity

We still -----
--------------wage war
--------------- kill without remorse
----------------consume without limits
watch others -----------
-----------------hate,
----------------- starve,
---------------- die of disease
----------------hide in fear
We look-----------
----------over our shoulders
but never look-----------
-------------in the face
of those----
-------- we hurt
--------------those we lie to
-----------------those we ignore

We are ----------
----------no closer
after 2000 years

--------------to our brother
--------------------to our source
------------to our Gods
--------------to our hearts
crying out
The voice----------
------------- in the wilderness
stll has not reached ------
---------our ears,
-------------our mouths
--------------our souls.

We have expanded-----------
---------our resources
--------- our knowledge
extended our reach-----------
across -------------
------- our world
-------- our universe
---------------- the unimaginable reaches
of time and space
but we still----------
can not reach----------
--------------our fellow man
---------------our inner feelings
--------------the spirit of our being
that which brought it
-------------------into existence.
The beast within us----------
still yearns-------
--------- to be free
struggles-------
------------- to get out
longs---------------
--------------- to be recognized.
We beat it back ---------
---------with logic
whip it into submission-------------
----------------with religion
-------------- calls to duty

but mostly-------------
--------- ignore it
as a unpleasnt reminder
of a not so recent past-----------
that still linger------
-------- glows
in the dark caverns
------------of our inhumanity.

Until----------
we can hug each other
as children---------- in a childs world
-------------without embarrassment
----------------without the uneasiness of personal contact
-------------------without the naked feeling of insecurety
The beast will remain----------------
----------------wild and untamed
------------hesitant and suspicioius
-----------------scared and lonely.
He will--------
-------- watch the TV
-------------- boot his computer
-------------- watch his world
-----------------for a sign,
--------------------a clue
---------------------an invitation
to the celebration---------
that lays---------
------------ within his heart
but far out of-------
--------- his reach.

T. P. Prince

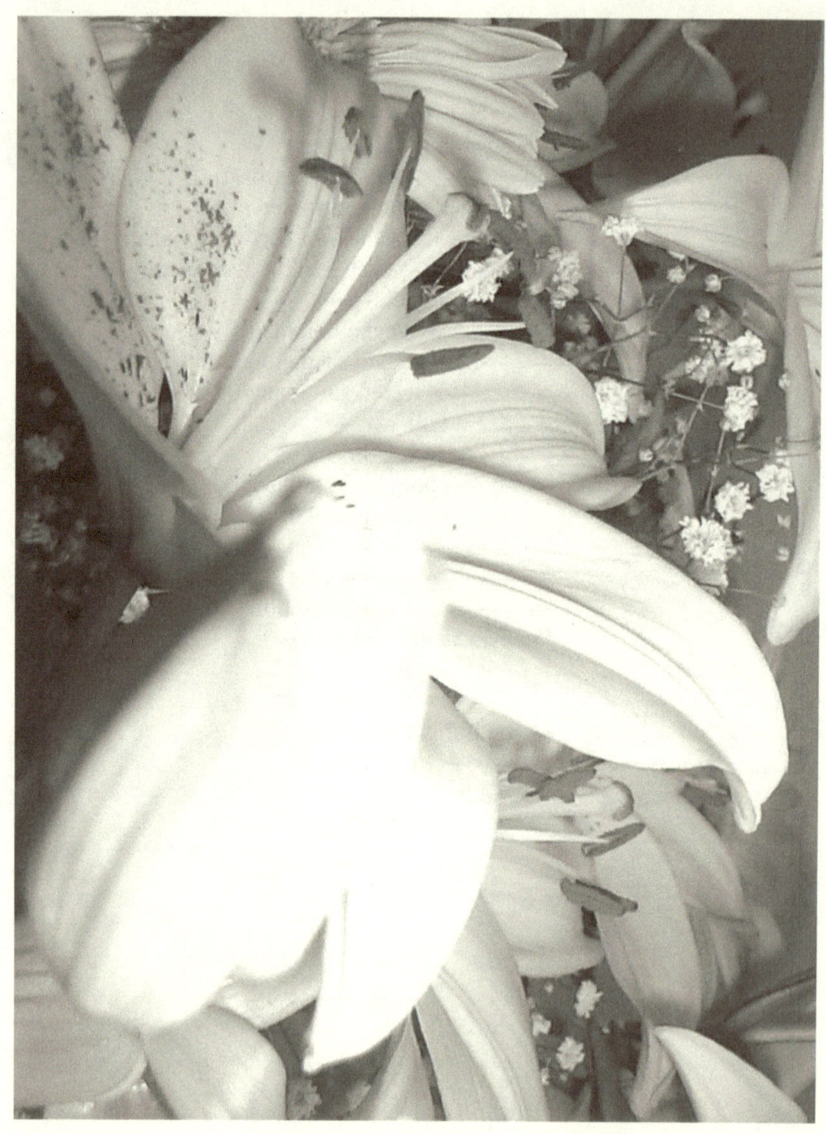

# age

We laugh-----------
in its face ---------when we are young
Long for it----------
when we are ------------denied
Lie about it--------
when we are--------too young, too old too far gone
Fight it---------
when caught---------- in the middle
overcome ----------by it
in the end.

It is both -----------our friend
--------- our foe.
It allows us----- to grow
enables us------- to learn
measures our--------
very being.

It is ------------our constant reminder
of the temporal fragility
of our existence.
It gives us------------
both---------
--------------continuity and range
---------random brevity.

We expect it----------
to give us--------- peace
--------------contentment
------------comfort
at its end
it gives us-----------
------------nothing.

It silently------------- waits
for us
-----------to admit
-------------to accept

------------to relinquish
the things-----------
that it has shown us
throughout------------
its persistent passing.

It will leave us---------
in the end
with the final---------
most definitive question
it has ever asked
during its playful passing

What------------
do you have left--------
that I ---------
can not----------
take away.

*helen-lorrraine-sandy*

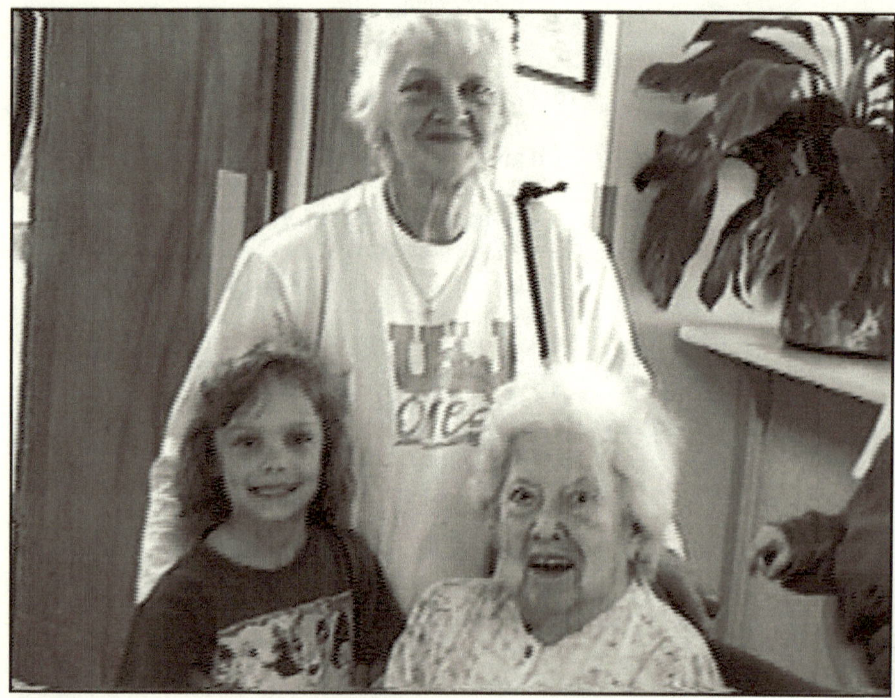

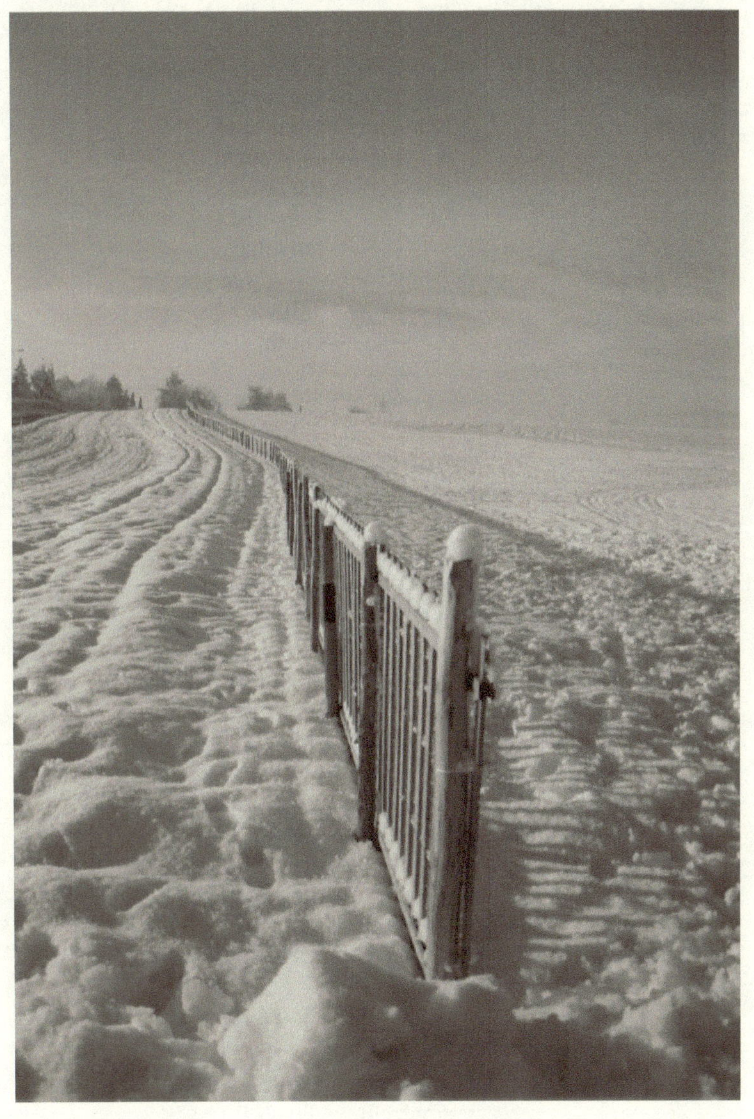

# *Lost child*

nervous stomach------------ dancing
mid gas and emptiness
to a loud familiar tune
of nights---------- spent
searching the road
for -------------my place
---------------anyplace
that will bring back-------- that glimpse
------------of hope,
---------- faith
------------love
that used to glow---------
like the tail light
of destiny's coach
giving direction -----------through
-------------the foggy logic
------------the crooked kindness
-----------the glaring truth.

he has nearly always-----------
----------------felt lost
among ----------the compromises
-------------the selfishness
--------------the prosperity
-------------the great silence
it takes to feed these beasts.
they have grown gigantic
----------on the silence he exports
--------------on the turning of the head
when the time comes to speak out
so that----------- pride and shame
can be swallowed
together------
without----------having to look
--------------in the hopeful faces
---------- of the children
----------- other unfortunate prey.

the less time ----------we have
the more ---------we waste

the greater the need-----------
--------------the less we share
without hope---------------
we only cultivate-----------
----------------despair.

hope-------
------------------ is in
the smile of a stranger
---------namelessly passing
the curious child
--------------endlessly asking
the beauty of a thigh
-------------in the sun basking
the kiss of a loved one
-----------eternally lasting.

T. P.

Prince

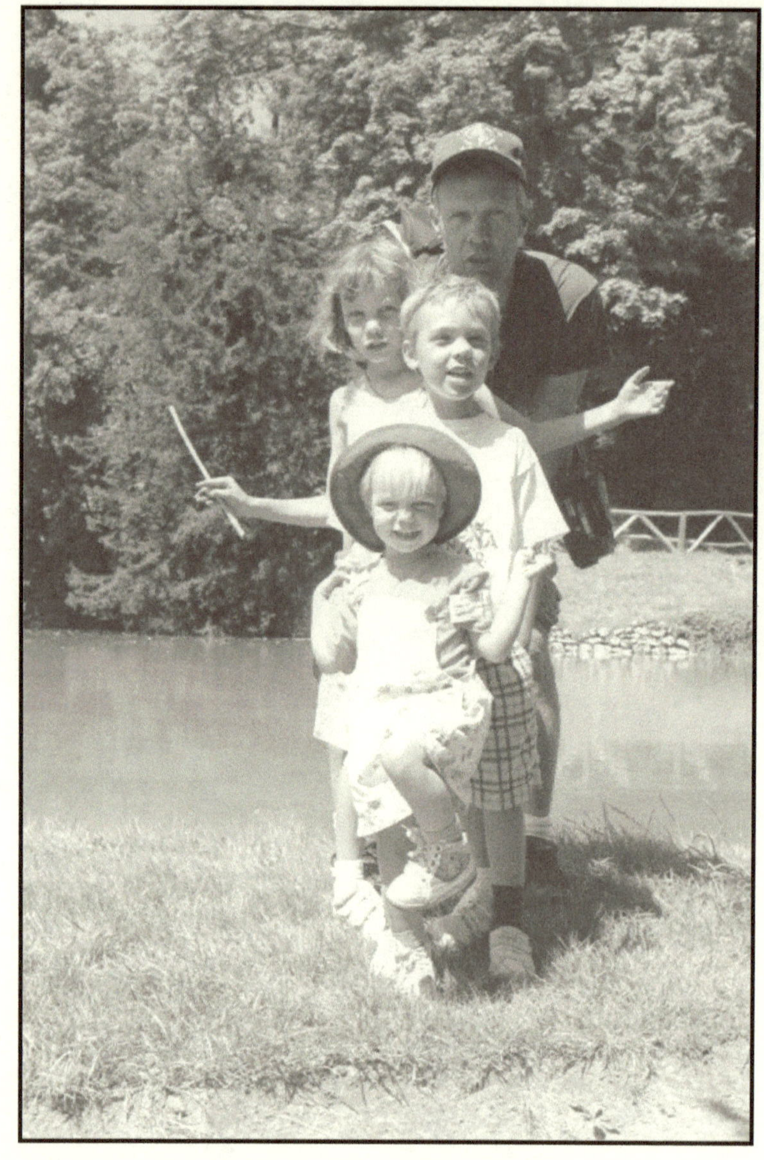

# take a chance?

nothing---------
is------------ not the answer
silence-------------
is not golden-
---------not the reply of choice-
it is a cautious negation
of all thought and feeling

No matter what------------
I will say
I will be--------- at fault
I will be----------- in trouble
I will be misunderstood
Why should I ------
----------say anything?
Why risk -------------the flings and arrows
--------Take a chance on truth?
-------Take a chance on you?
---------Take a chance on me?

We can survive ------------with ignorance
but can we suffer----------
----------The Truth?

We are all---------------
-------- alike
---------- in this together
Our hearts pump------
----- the same blood
------in the same direction
but not-------------
-------- with the same force.

If I give you----------- the knife
to cut my bonds
How will I know ---------
you will not---------

-----------cut my throat?
I can survive------
---------- the unhappiness
------------the loneliness
-----------the longings
---------the doubt
--------------- fear
But------------
can I survive---------------
-----------The laughter
------------pointing fingers
------------- wide eyed disbelief
---------------- ridicule
the compassionless rejection of---------------
------------- my heart
-------------my soul
-----------my frailty
---------------shortcomings
the unwashed nakedness
-------------of my very being?

If we ----------
can not walk------------
bodily naked in warm sunlight
with the ones we love
How can we expect--------------
to walk with our bare being exposed
to the scopes of those----------
---------- we love
--------------admire
------------- fear
-----------those we hate.

"coming together" tpprince 1989

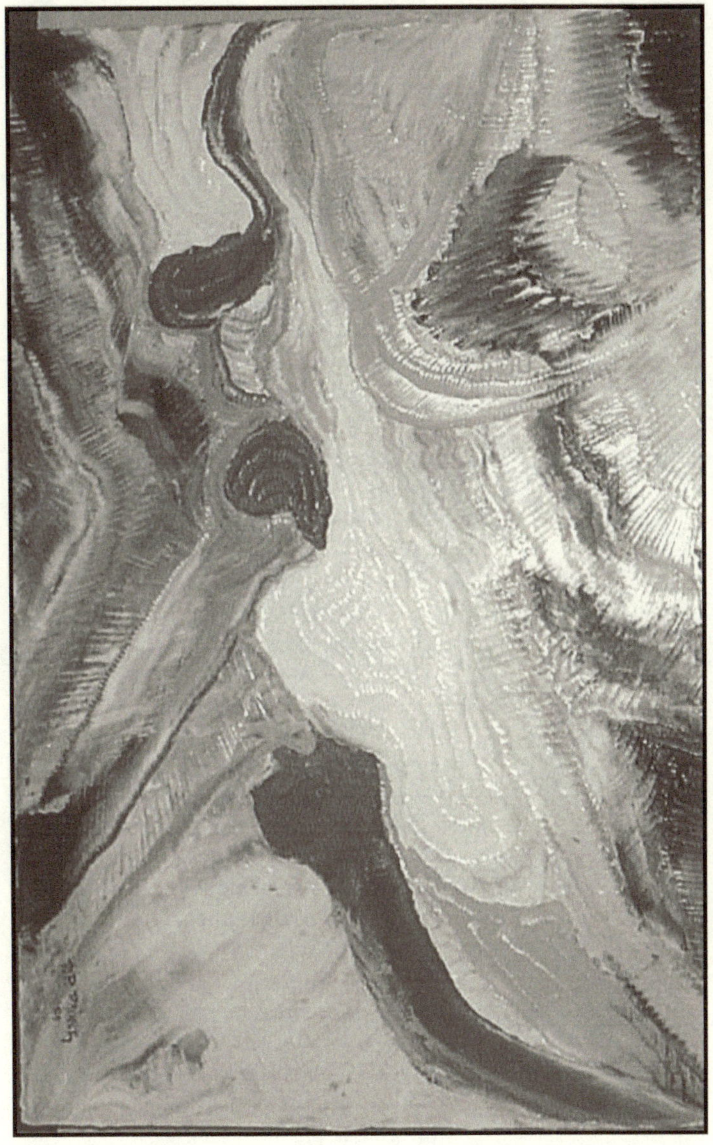

# hogwarts

in the mist of life
sometimes-----------
------------- our minds
find --------
---------------a clearing
a place through-------------
-------------- the fog
---------------the disappointment
------------ the bullshit
beyond --------------------
-------------------constant contradictions

a place of-------------
-------------- excitement
------------- intrigue
a place-----------------
--------- of rest
a sign -----
-------------of hope
a ray --------------
-------------of unmolested sunlight

we can glimpse -----------
------------the golden snitch
----------flying through the rain
-----------effortlessly skirting
---------------- dismal clouds
-------------- dissappointment
giving us a direction
------------to pursue
-----------to dreams
----------to forget
----------our fears
-----------our pains
offering some means
of setting aside---------------
-------------our losses
--------------our crushed ambitions

---------------our obese inabilities
-----------------to change
,-------------to cure
----------- to mend
the ills --------
--------of our world
the terminal inflictions----------------
that incompasitate
our very souls.

escape ----------------------
------to the safe place
find -----------------
----------the wings to rest
your weary soul

then-------------- tommorrow
we shall not only-----
--------- live
---------- fight again
but -----------------maybe find
the way ---------
to soar---------------
-------------------------on our magical brooms
and light the way home---------------.
----------------------------with a wand
and a------------ word.

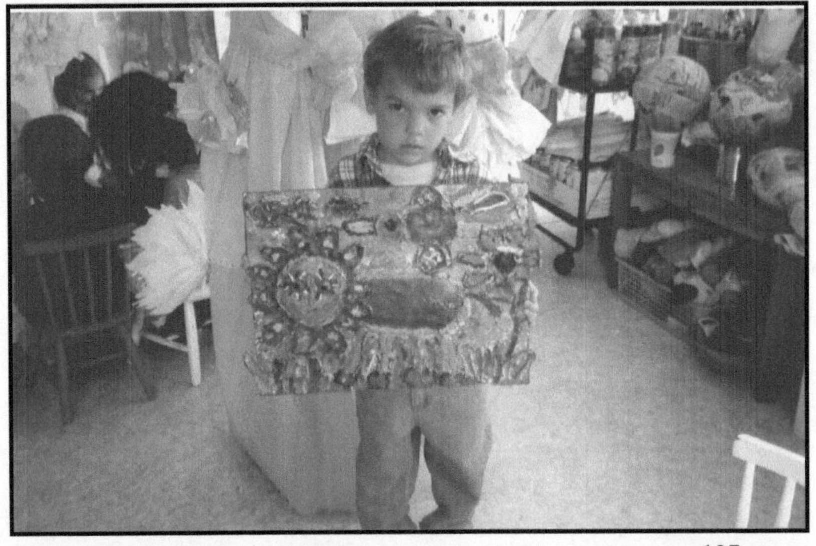

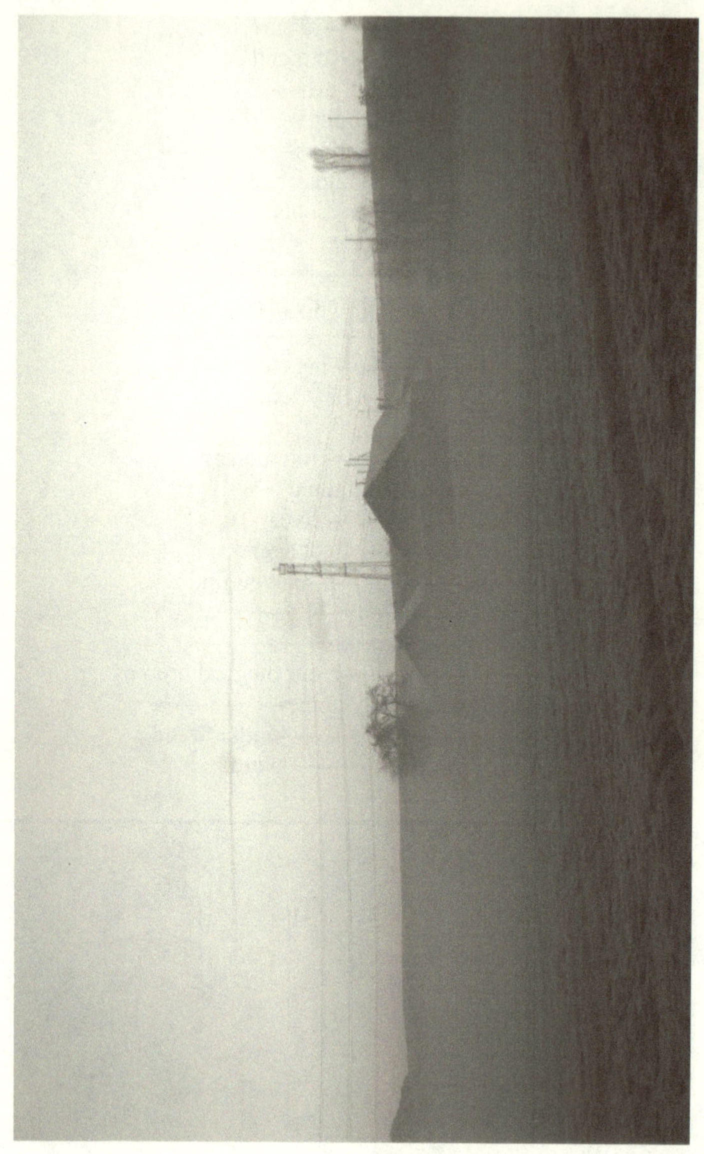

# *seriously*

don't take it too-------
I'm not joking
please take me-------
please consider me-------
He was injured-------

What does it all mean?
I could use some serious laughter!
I was only poking fun
and she took me------
We can have serious sex
but not serious violence.
People cover  eyes
during a a sex scene
but open  eyes wide  for
butal killing
sadistic torture
tragic accidents.
Is death and injury
not as personal as
making love in a hammock.

Why do we cover our eyes
at the prolification
of life
and yet----------
are messmerized by---------
-------------the slaughter
----------the dismembering
-------------the mental cruelty
of our fellow man?

perhaps--------------
we can't distance ourselves from--------
------------ intimacy
----------- beauty
----------- uncontolable urges
------------- distant drums
that call to-----------
------- our hearts

---------our minds
-------- our spirits.

perhaps-----------
somehow-----------
we equate ourselves
too closely with--------
-----------the coming together
-----------of nature
----------the species
---------warm flesh
---------- flowing juices
-------uncontrolable emotional fullfillment.

unable to harden ourselves
with the same calouses
that we use to
distance ourselves from----------
---------- inhumanity
----------- malilcious mayhem
----------compassionless neglect
--------suffering and death?

simply -----------
------- unable to
---------no desire
to distance ourselves----------- from pleasure
so we must ovoid -------------the implication
protect ourselves-----------
from our empty hearts and souls
longing for -----------
--------the fairy tale
------------ fulfillment
---------- the closest of contact
with other lost -----------searching souls

have we sold our rights
to walk in the Garden
-----------Unafraid

-----------Unprotected
---------un-noticed
------------unclothed
fragile-------------- yet
God-like?
Were we thrown out of the Gate-----------
or
-----------------just loose our way back.
.

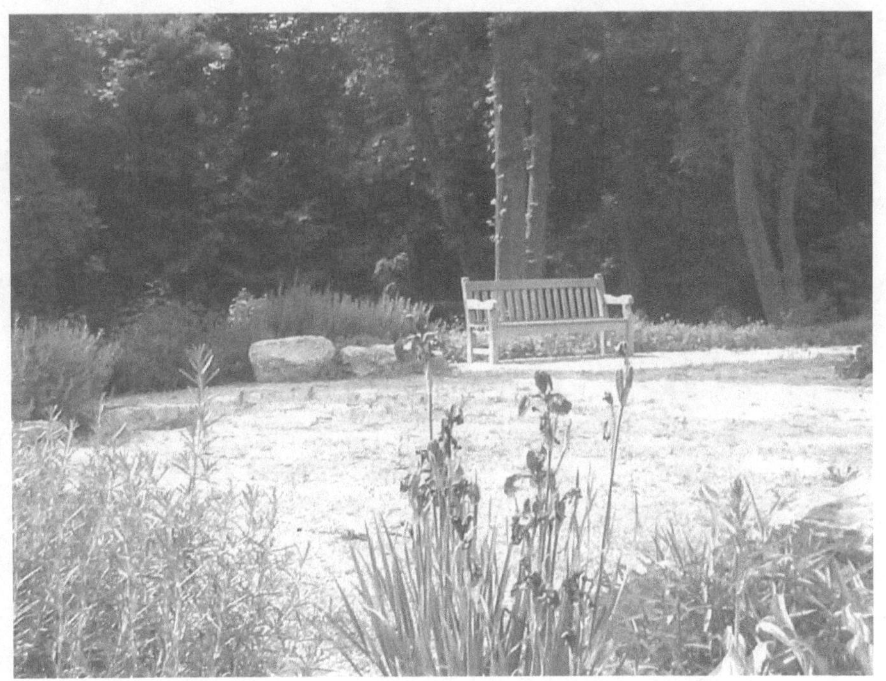

# The Auditor

We are lost?
we stare----------------- squint
looking -----------beyond the lark.
smell--------- the pity of The Maker
sense ----------the lack of impotence.

we seek---------- to make ourselves
------------ the very things
---------we fear
---------detest
the perfectionist curse
haunts us-----------------
----------------------around darkened corners
laughs at us----------------
as we proclaim victory
in the wrestle with the wind.

I will love you------------
only-----------
If you love me.

I will protect you-----------
if -----------you are loyal
to my ---------dogma
------------ authority
to ------------my bidding
----------my plan
of existence.

I will help you-----------
if------------- you
--------------sacrifice yourself
---------follow without--------
-----------complaint
---------question
----------direction
-----------hesitation.

I will be------------ jealous
----------------consuming
-------------patronising
-----------uplifting
-----------unfaltering.

until--------------
the time comes--------
to relieve------------ the boredom
promote----------- another
advance ----------the wheel
bury ------------the past
till-----------
the clock---------
strikes-------------- another hour.

A dim view-----------
floats -------------through
a dusty window
giving ------------a glimpse
of --------------
---------past mistakes,
-----------miscalculations
in the simple balance
between ------------our summation
of Godly expectation-----------
and---------------
human endowments.

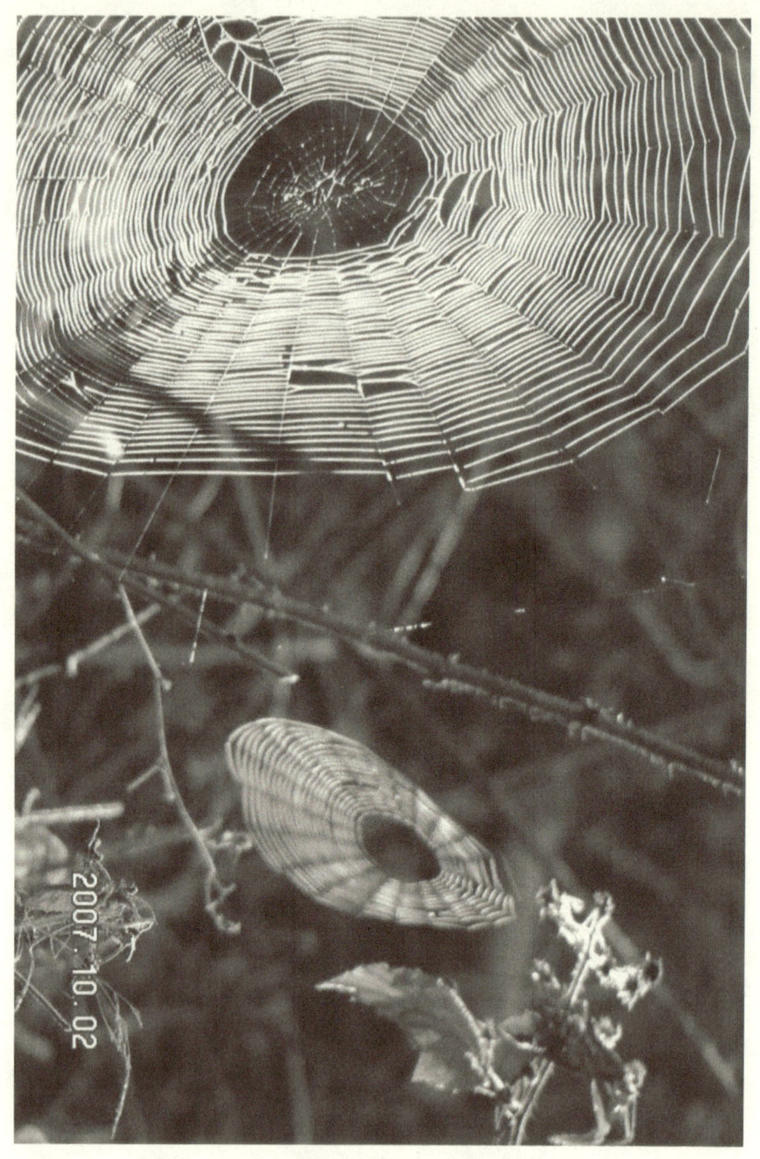
2007.10.02

# *Hair vs Nair*

It changes-------
---------- color
----------- location
-----------our minds
------------ attitudes

the bearded lady------------
doesn't sing
doesn't----------- model lipstick

It marks ------------our existence
like rings a trees
It invades----------- our private part
---------our ears
defiently sticking out
in ambarrasing directions
our eyes are invades---------------- by unruly lashes
and savage brows
our noses-------------
sprout bristles to trap
-------------runny discharges
----------- clingy stubborn boogers.
You wipe them
but they still hang---------
in discusting places
in an effort---------
to discredit your authority
making you look foolish
again

other places-------------
trap bodily refuse
in the same manner
but are
not visible to--------------
the questioning eye------------
that examines our faulty existence.

we -----------pluck them
------------wax them

-----------cut them
------------shave them
----------burn them
----------color them
-------------electrocute them
-----------disolve them in acid
but-----------
like weeds ---------
they won't be denied
they passively come back
without hate----------- vengeance
they want------------ nothing
they will take----------- nothing
it is our war---------
not theirs

they tell our story------------
a story--------- we don't wish to hear
they remind us----------- of our past
they speak---------- of the limits
------------of our future
they underline-------------
weaknesses--------
our inability to stand ----------alone
our fear to accept -------------ourselves
as we are.

We make----------- the most deadly
of our self centered assumptions

It is our body
we------------- control it
we --------------reign
now------------- forever---

Till death -----------
-----do we part.

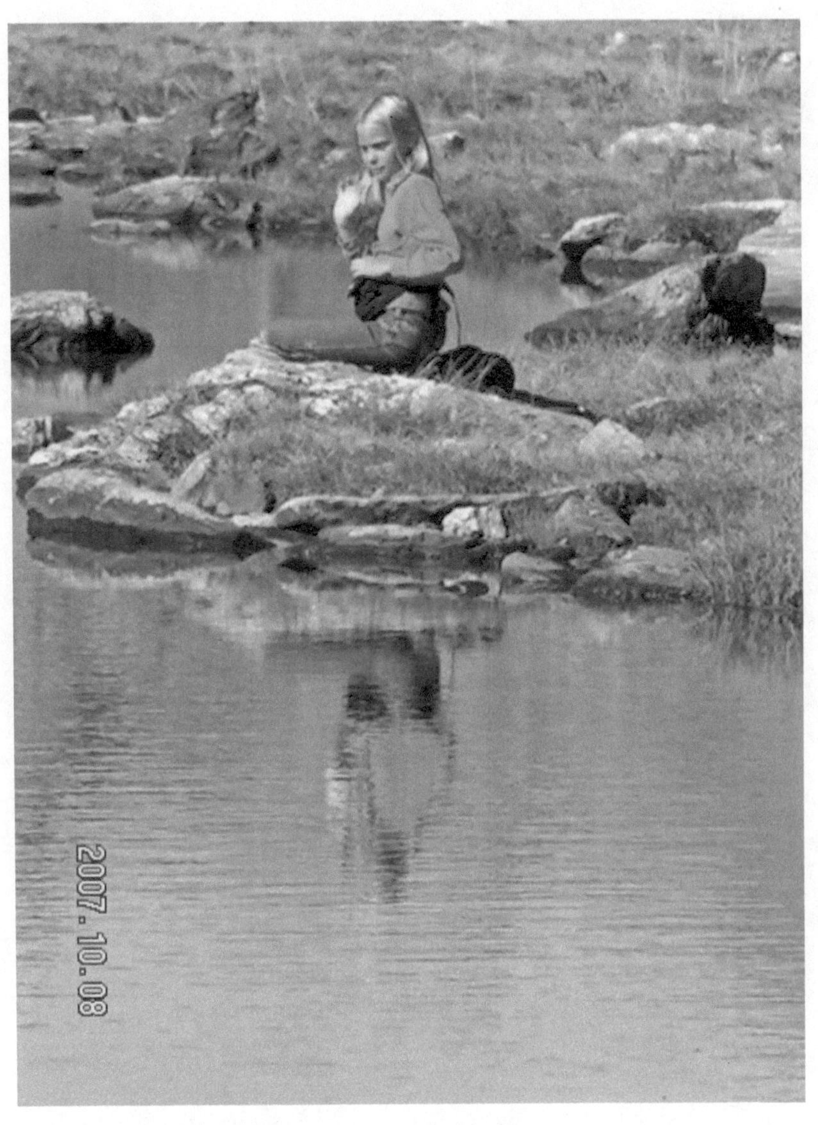
2007.10.08

# follow directions

the balls float --------
--------amoung the tree tops
children unseen-------
------ cock heads
to watch ---------
to dream---------
if --------
---it makes it
through the trees.
they all return -------------to earth
and prepare------------
------- for the next launch

window breezes brush-----------
---------face----------- hair
but end up-----------
-------------- nowhere
they are absorbed--------
-------- in the walls
that protect us?----------
from the uncontrollable changes
----------- of the seasons
from the variety
------------of natural unpredictability.

We try to perfect-----------
---------our climate
-------------our insatiable existence

the plan ------------- by nature
is to ultimately fail
what have we----------
----------to win?
----------to lose?
The play is------------ the key
can't win if---------- you don't play
can't lose if-------- you don't quit
don't need --------faith
if you're given---------
The Answer.

How else----------- could it
all work?
How would you
design ----------
the universe?
How would you
deal------
------ with eternity?
Heaven?
Pretty absurd
What would you do there
after ----------the first week
-------------the first year
-------------------the first millennium?

Look at the child-----------
as he plays ----
-------his heart
The game ----------
only limited
by-------------- his hunger
--------------his fatigue
--------------his imagination
------------his parents.
He has no need
to know-------------
-----------------the score
-----------the rules of nature
----------the prise to gain
-----------the glory of victory
------------the agony of defeat
how ---------to cheat
----------to lie
-----------to save face
where -------
-------to pass blame
when -----
----to cash in the chips.
If he likes the game-----------
-------------he plays
when he tires---------
------------he quits

the outcome-----------
---------------quickly forgotten
to ready a place-----------
for the next to begin.

to keep the game
a simple part
of the heart
is the only direction
written on the inside of
his umbilical cord.

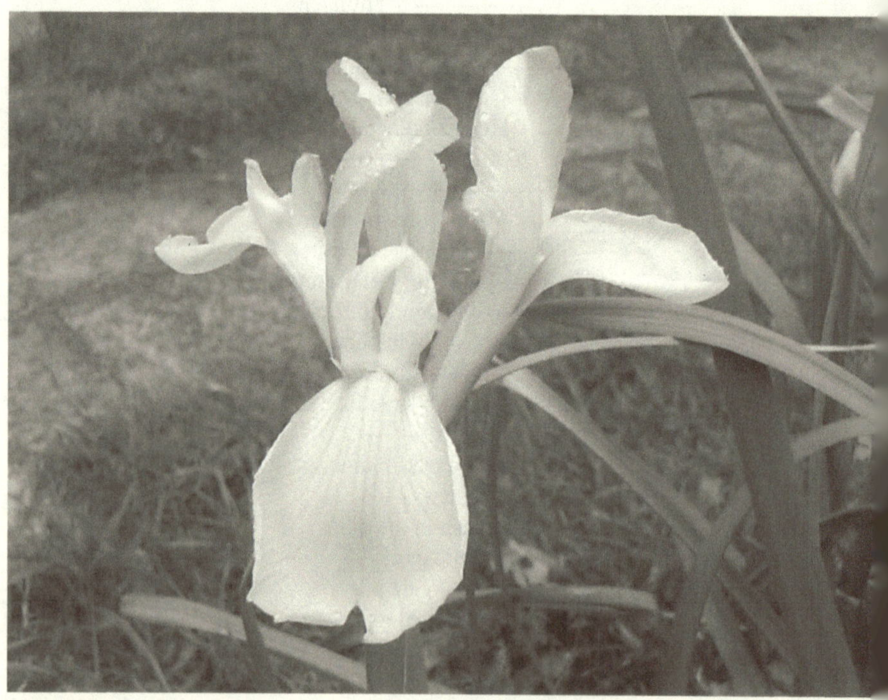

# for never after

it spills--------
down  from  open mouths
it rains--------
through the thickest forest
seeps into------
---------unassailable cracks
--------seamless securety vaults.

Burning our eyes
burying our hearts-----
in an inundation of regret
sealing-------
our illusory dooms-----
in the total darkness of
-----------radical subversion
---------orthodox dogmatics
steadfast adherrance to---------
biblical reverberations
------------void of reason
delineated to superceed being.

Forever  is----
--the battle cry
Forever----------
the reason to fight on
against-----------
-----------disparity
--------insensitivity
-----------ambiguity.

In the forever---------
life will--------
give us ---------justice
---------peace
-----------reward
---------reason.

There is no---------

---------reward
for action --------
------------done for reward
Just as------
------ there is no reward
-------for the wicked
who mirror the same motive
for achieving----------
-----------desired ends
-------------self gain

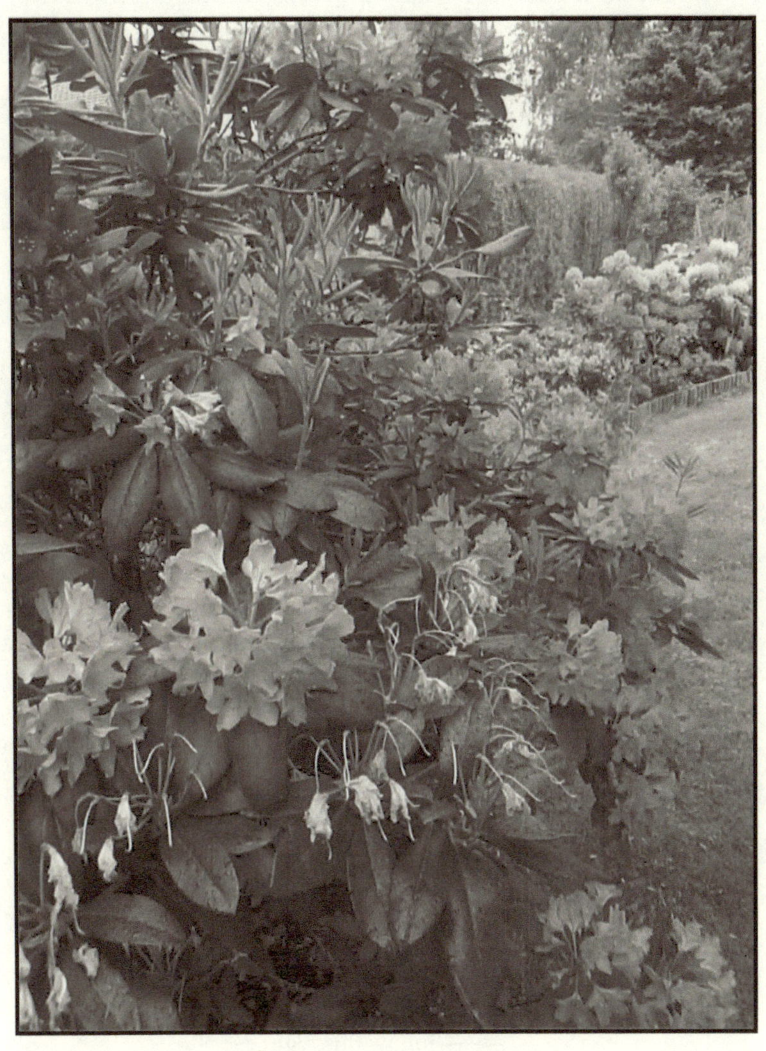

# yearn to learn

find the secret-------------
---------to being
------------seeing
go along with-------
open searing searching hearts
that delights---------
----------in the new
--------the untried
---------the unsafe
----------the unknown
be alert to-----------------
stumbling blocks-----
----------that trip minds
------------ camouflage souls
---------------with trivial facts
----------- mundane duties
that can neither-------------
--------- advance the center
-----------the struggling spirit
in its quest for achievement

People might tell you-------
you must-------
-------------get this done
------------read this treatise
----------know this slogan
------------pray this canon
-----------sing this anthem
-----------believe this theorem
-----------eat this vegetable
-----------drink this milk
--------follow this regime

It is good------------
----------- for you
-------------for us

----------for the world
All might be lost if -------
--------you don't adhere
-------------don't tow ------
------------the line of expectancy
That has kept our world
together for thousands of years.

do not ------------------
--------rock the boat
-------buck fate
-------temp the gods
-------upset the apple cart.

It has been -------
---------the fools

Who have advanced
the race
Not --------
--------the trainer
------------the time keeper
------------the judge
------------the advocates
--------the critiques.
without the meandering mutant
civilisation is lost
in its own excrements
with no place to put------
its gangly left foot.

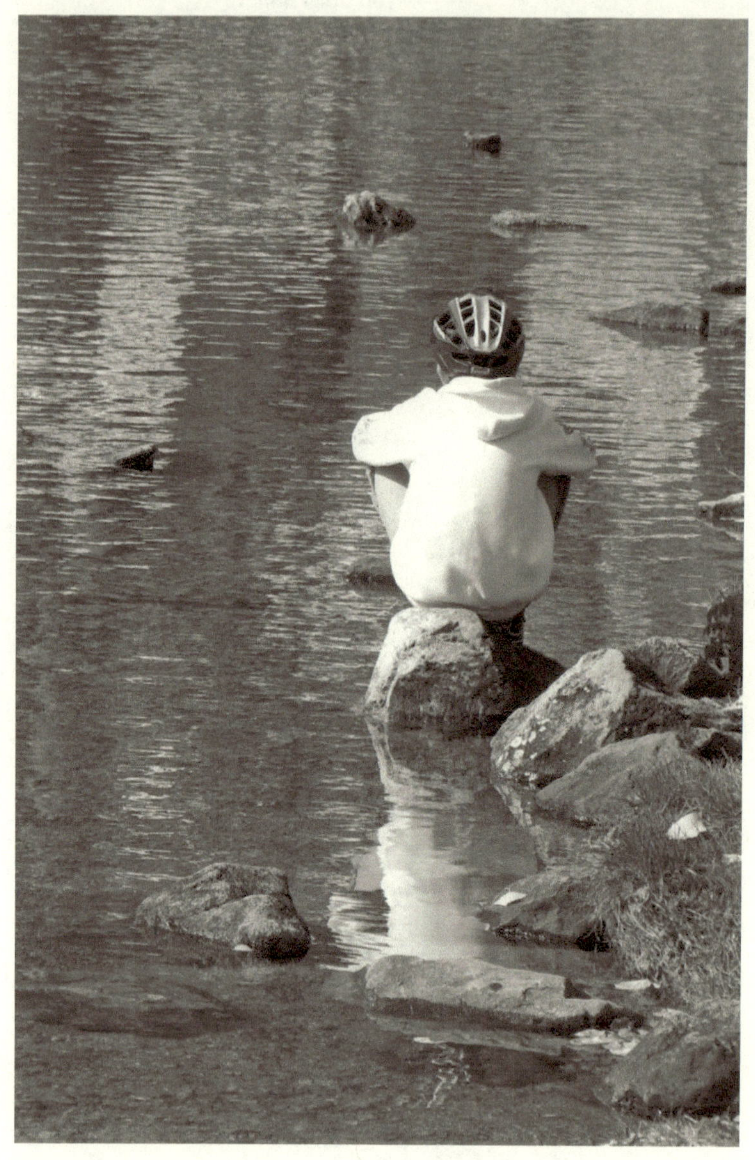

# Cold grey

Sputtering in the mist
barely inching off the tarmac
it attempts to take off.
Try again
Again--------
--------------------Again

Barren limbs bend and break
naked birds vainly attempt to shelter
behind frosted branches
white bitter and dormant

The engine staggers and stalls
bringing hopes to a gradual standstill
Somehow--------------
It isn't moving.. but it hasn't stopped
You see the lack of motion---------
but not the end
It has not truly stopped
It has not quit

You can see in your heart
The landing gears goodbye kiss to the ground
the flaps waving in the breeze
the wings rising through the ascent.

But it is still-------------
lost in the middle of the runway.
Motionless-------------
without---------- a sound.
------------direction
---------motivation

without ------------a clue
without-------- a hope.

From the birches --------------------
one of the condemned birds
leaves  bitter branches
to find the fleeting warmth
of the fading engine
He pecks at the fuselage
The tin beats echo through the lifeless craft
grey feathers ruffle again
the beak opens and he chirps
Softly but clearly toward the cockpit

After a long hesitation------
the engine slowly begins to revolve
burping and barking
the fire inside ignites
The craft returns to the runway
revving up
painting the wind with its defiant roar

The bird returns to its place on the branch
Watching and hoping
It knows death is coming
The craft tries to reach potential
the runway quickly dissolves
The grey plumes ruffle in the disturbance
as the wheels break the dementors kiss

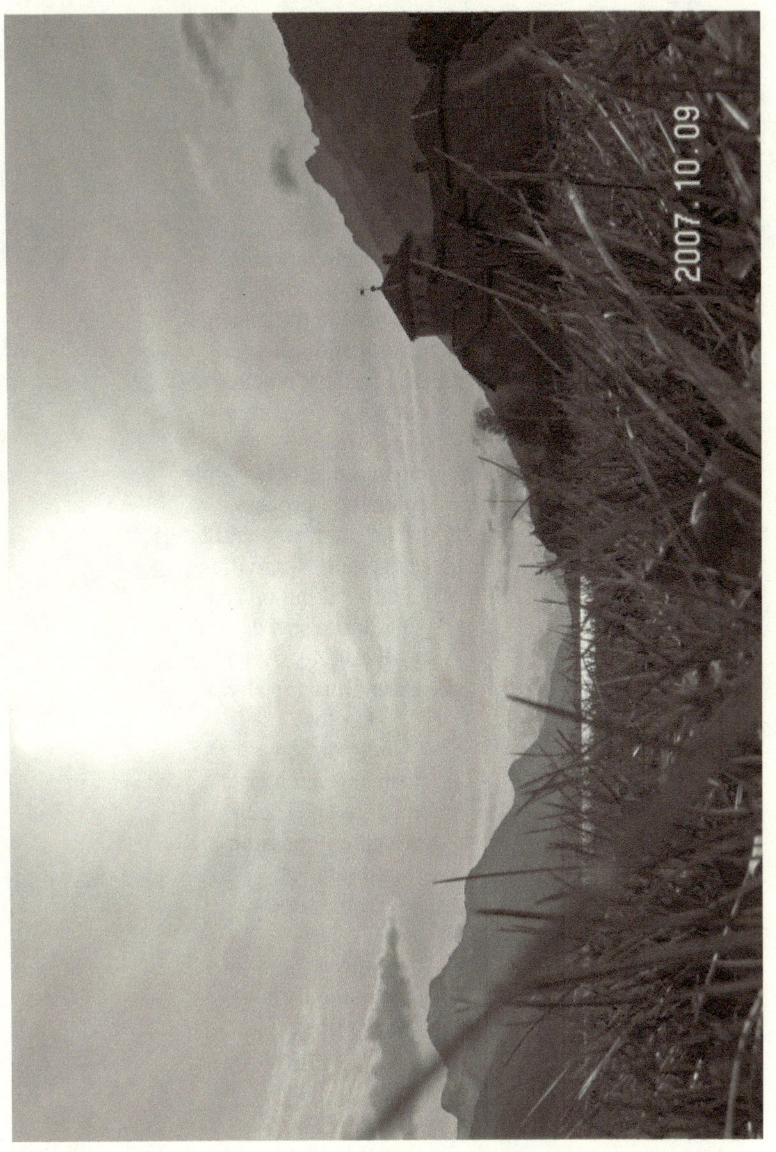
2007.10.09

# Acclimation

Can we-----

find our way
back
again to the future
to the light
to the warmth
Do the embers still
faintly glow
somewhere in the distant
corners of our hearts
in the furthest reaches
of our souls gone ascew

the long and nearly invisible
aclimation process
slowly turned out hearts and lungs
into huge hollow cavities
inefficiently taking up space
and more space
so we might survive
the ascent into the abyss
but lose
our passion
lose our laughter
our sight and touch
lose our compassion
our smiles
lose all hope.

who is…
the enemy?
who will be …
the comrade?
the saviour
the destroyer.
who can…
love
who cannot..
endure?

who can care
…not despair?
who will understand
be they not understood

can we …
find our way?
must we…
choose to stay
the way we are
caring less each day
acclimating ourselves
to the cold
the useless burdens
of mistrust
covering one's ass
in case things go astray

bearing the souls of others
while locking our own
in a secret Luxembourg vault
with numbers and no names
to protect us from
anyone…
searching for the truth
searching a path
searching the way
to our hearts
to our minds
to our souls.

We cannot find a direction
must less a path
We have trouble hearing
the truth
We are always straining our ears
to try to pick up
the muffle of a lie
of a failure
of a concession
of an imperfection---
not from ourselves
but from those around us.

We have acclimated ourselves
to lies
to callousness
to self-pity
to tears
to fears
to loneliness
.
to find any hint of goodness
our chests have expanded
our heads have ballooned
our hearts have hollowed
stretching to limits
to try …
to take advantage
of the faintest
breath
of true sharing and trust.

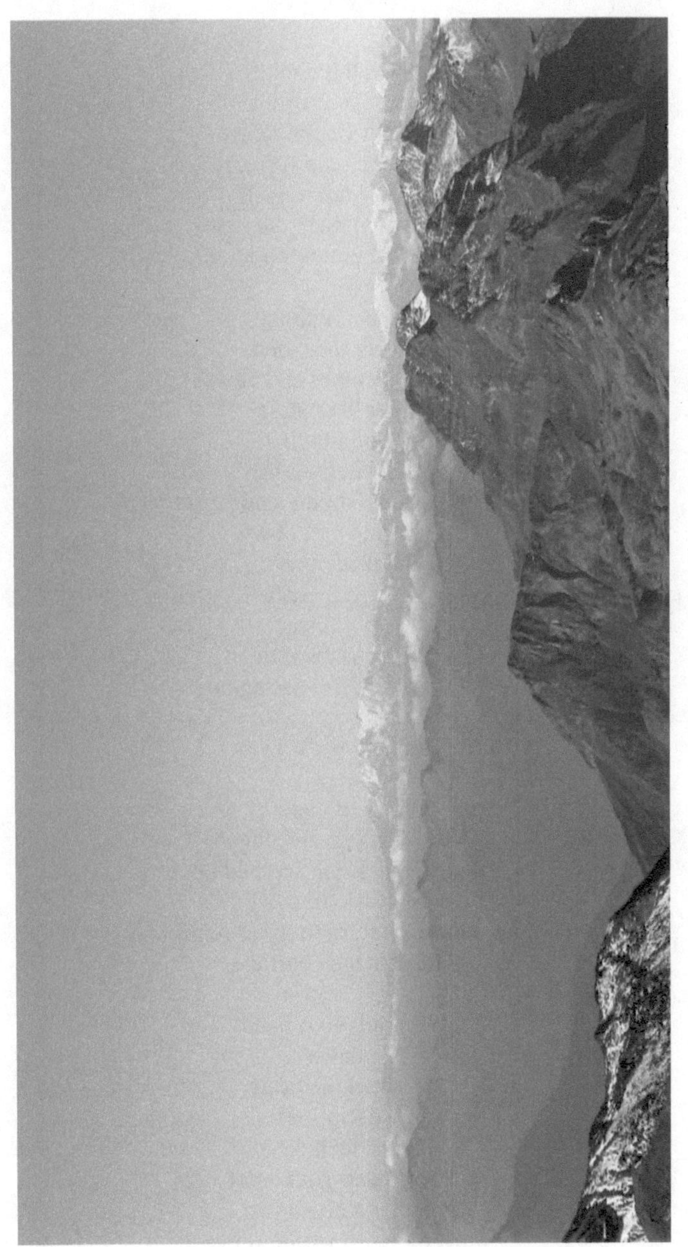

# *knew*

Feel the light,
taste the warmth
Wet your finger before
You touch the surface
Careful not to spill
Slowly approach the new
Hesitate but not too long

Expect nothing
Except the worst
Before it comes and clogs
Your happiness
Good faith
Kind intentions
With disappointment and regret
Bringing you down
To that place you…….
…………hate
……….fear
never wanted to
………………. see again

Turn and walk away
before……….
It is too late
Your feathers are singed
Your feelings are scraped up
Your heart is out to dry……
Your defences return to try to reinforce
The damaged barriers.

You pull your hand
…..away
re-chain the heart
severely discipline ………
your feelings.
Reprimand your heart
for not first checking…..
with General intelligence.

Reality returns from behind the tree
Putting the pants of the past
Back in its place.
The light is still bright
It radiates warmth
Your hand slowly reaches out
And the spit on your finger
..................sizzles

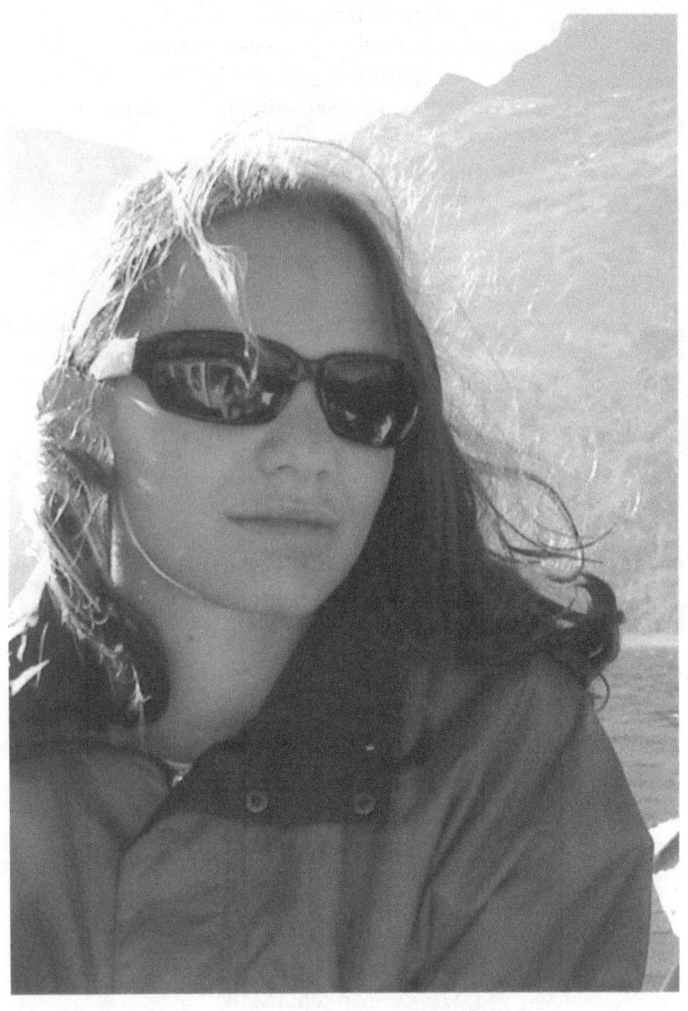

# Baghdad Bones

falling relentlessly over
the pathetic path
obscuring the envisioned....

planned, promoted and pillaged
by expectations—grandiose desires
sons of liberators look up
to the aspirations of disappointing generations

the boomers tried to followed the ----
the footsteps of the fathers
into the storm of mistakes and trepidations
that surrounded the path to immortality

alas....
they are not the chosen few
to real sense of hope and duty
they confused a call to glory....
with a cry for help---
answering a plea for recognition
with a call for battle.

Doubt rains down bullets of tears
Obscuring the battlefield
With "les nuages" of fear.

Can anyone find an honest end
To justify such ruthless means?

Like a child's determined victory
to avoid spinach
Will the mere strength of will
Be enough to mend
Such hideous tears
In the membranous wounded skin
That covers the sensitive sense
Of our shared humanity.

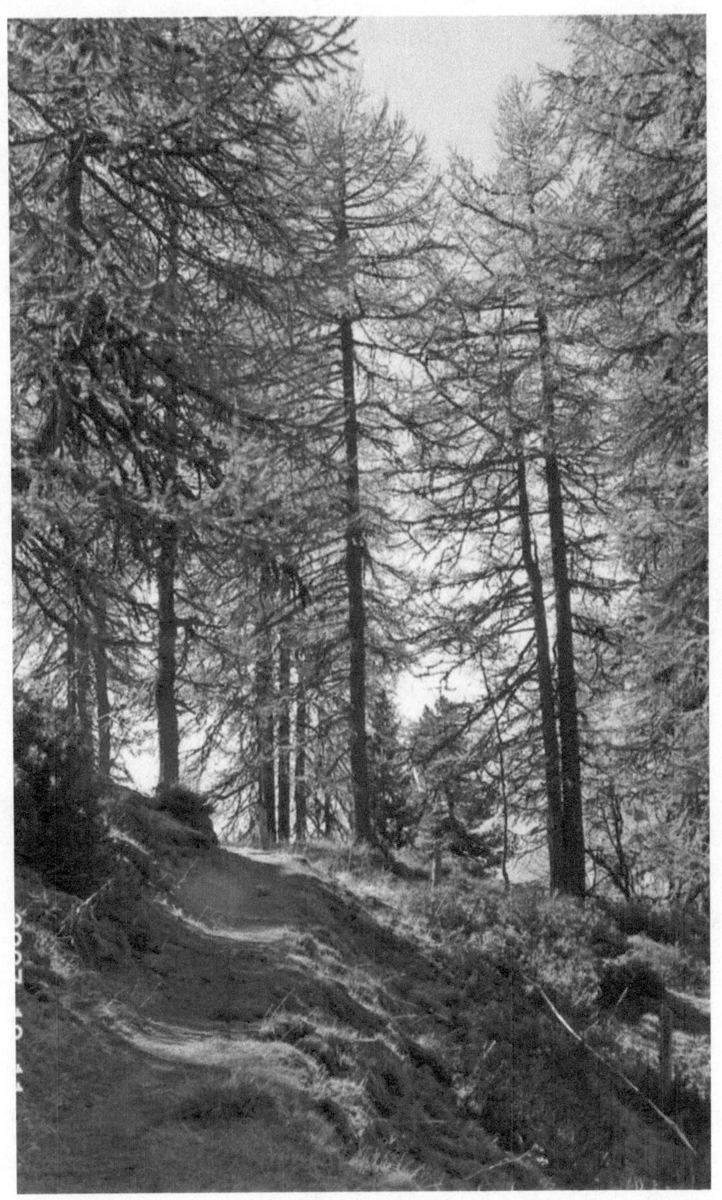

# Carmel Shake

*(Sharm el Sheikh)*

warm dark
flowing and intense
melting down the river of kings
distributing salt and sugar
along the wind torn banls
turning dessert gold to emerald
shaded peaceful nourishment.

like the Nile fighting the sun
they battle the harsh environment
of demanding needs
and limited resources
covering themselves in
faith ….
Belief…
in trust
and in love
against
the glaring sun
animalistic desires
selfish pride.

burka barriers …
ward off
base desires…
unrelenting longings….
capable of spiritual corruption
heavenly destruction

one seldom falls victim to temptations
of unknown or unseen origin.

if one sets thoughts to paradise
they cannot be left to dwell in hell.
in loving our neighbours ..
our brothers

we cannot covet
his heart and breath.
sharing hope…
wishing others happiness
leaves no place
no time…
to abuse
or deceive his soul.

is aiding our fellow man not
our own cry for help?

we administer to our own
curses and wounds
when we aid our brothers.

turn not away from the flaws of others
for they reflect our own wounded hearts.

smile through the hardships
the plagues
the doubts
give thanks..
for the opportunities of hope
that guide you
through the fallacies of pleasure
introducing you to trials of faith
the temporal timber of dreams and disappointment
break bread
with the true source of the River.

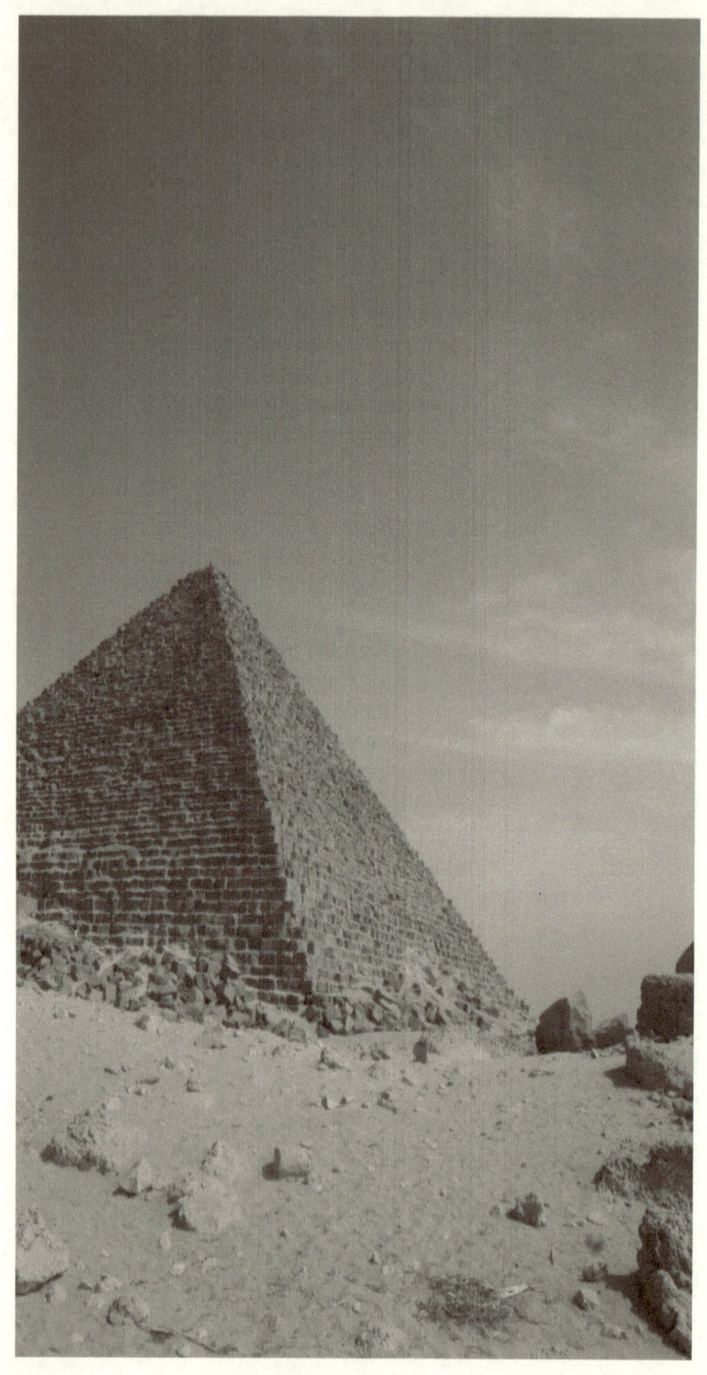

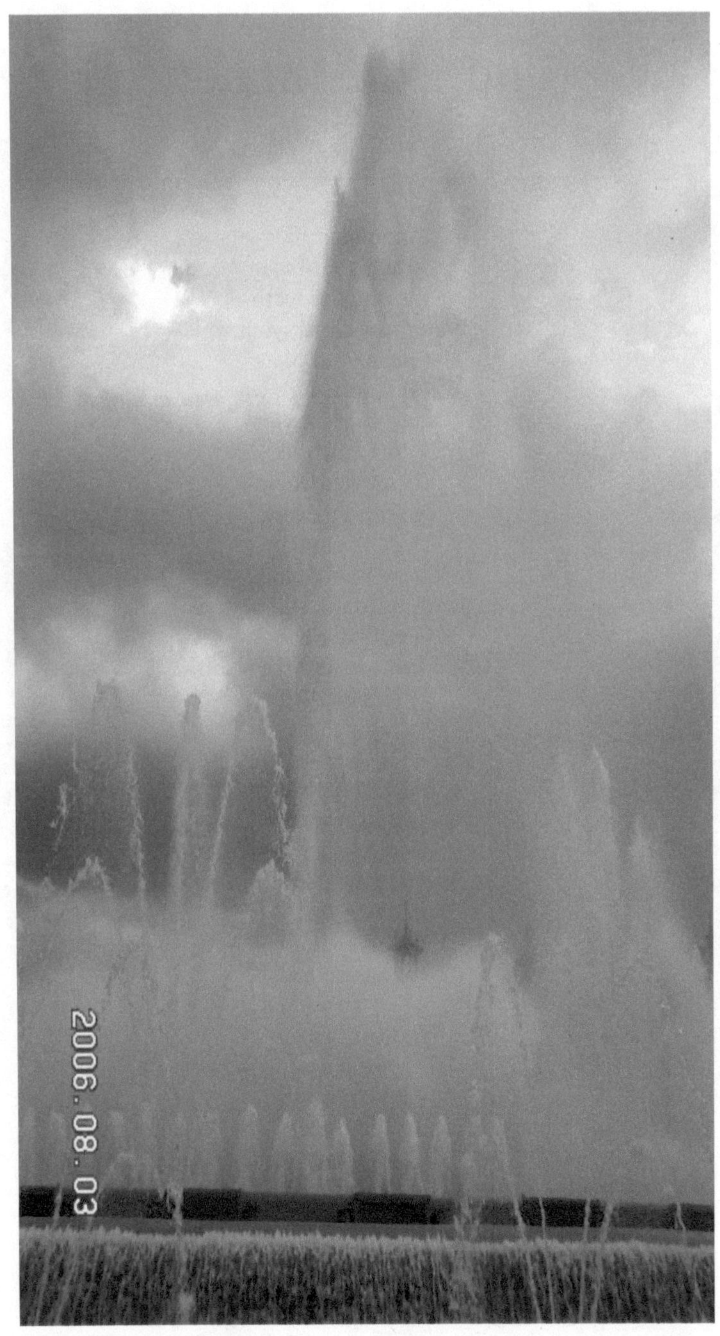
2006.08.03

# Under the Influence

Comb your hair—
wash your face-
brush your teeth
Eat your peas-finish your milk-
clean your plate
Put your feet down
-say your prayers-
play outside
Clean your room-
your homework-
go to church
Change your cloths-
do the dishes-take out the trash-
wash your hands
Go to bed-turn out the lights-
go to sleep-get up

Eat—eat-eat-
sleep-sleep-sleep-
Run-run-run—
work work work-
calm down-calm down calm down.

It has no beginning—
it has no end.

We learn-we teach-
we obey-
we command
We force-
we persuade
we adhere
we struggle
and fail

We force our mind….-
our thoughts-
our feelings

Never really knowing …..
our own minds,
true thoughts….,
real feelings.

we assume to know those of others
better than our own?
Spare the rod and spoil the child
Be a parent not a friend
-force and fear motivates best-
forget kindness and understanding
They only complicate
get in the way of discipline.

Love and understanding only get in the way.
They are not aggressive enough to work here.
People will only ignore kindness
and ovoid understanding.
crush the will them under combat boots.

what is for the best
who decides .
we know what is best for others
we do not know
what is best for ourselves.
We are influenced by the sound of the wind in our ears,
the fear in our hearts
The hand that rocks the cradle—
the dictator who rules the world
Study math-physics-science-business-Latin-law
Get the best scores-the highest grades
Attend the best schools—make the most money
Then take it to your grave
Your final mark will be written in stone
at the head of your final resting place.
Will it be your epitaph?
Or that of the prevailing wind.

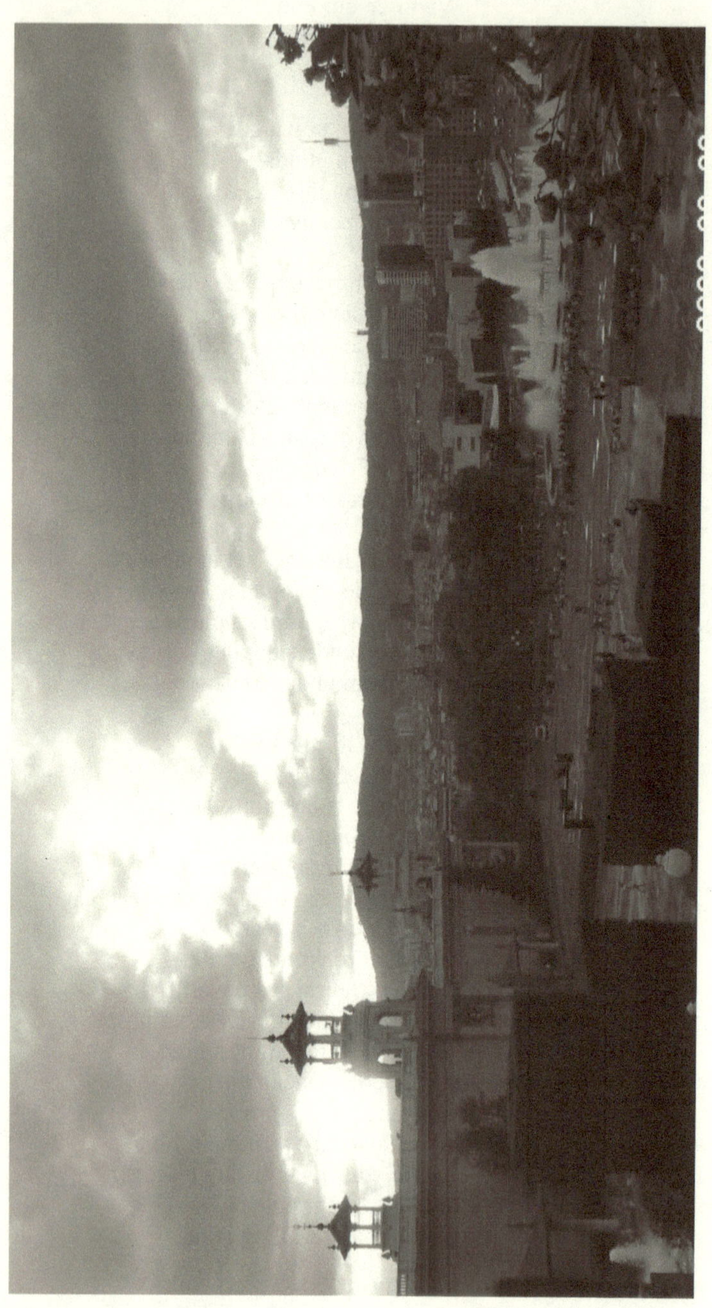

# *Hallwiller*

he miniscule flying insects
turn white against the burning candle
falling along-side the fiery flame
in hills of snowy cinders
they live in darkness searching for
the light and warmth
in which nature directs them against
all logic and reason to
a piery consumation of consentrated light
why do they search the illuminations
what is the hypnotic directive
that can neither be
denied, understood nor shared

growing up boring
losing ground to
fear and knowledge of
risks and insignificant gains that
should not be sought
should not be fought
should not be considered in
the equation of a natural existence
not be the measure of
justifiable motivation and action

at our deaths
do we head toward the light
the flaming fiery candle
that rescues us from
the darkness of the night
the ignorance of our existence
the inhumanity of
our selfish meagre expectations
bringing us to the next
level of being and knowing
or ------------is the light
the enemy
the scourging scoundrel
that pulls us toward it seductive light
only to zap us into a pile
of crispy snow-white cinders

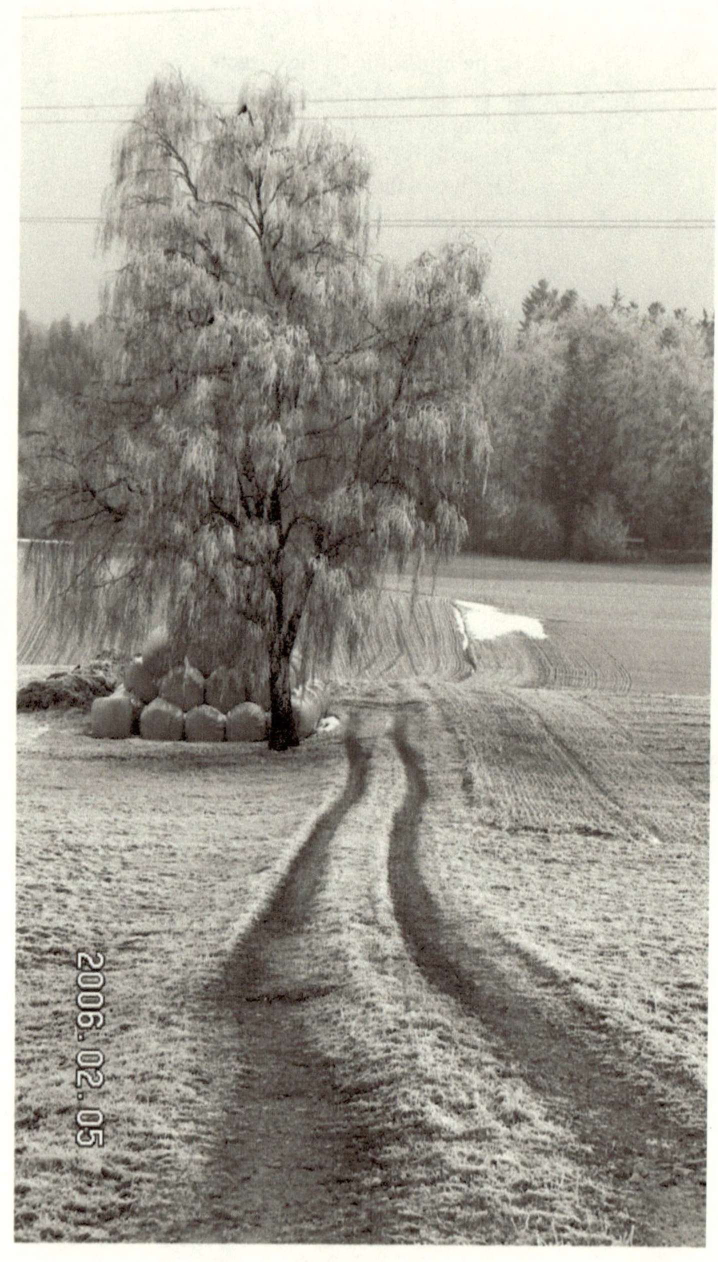
2006.02.05

# DAVOS

Across the great divide

*Lies the valley*
*… … … … … … ….. of ruins*
*The lives… … … … … …*
*… … … … … … … .. misplaced,*
*… … … … … … ….. abandoned*
*By well wishers on their way*
*To the promised land*
*Promises of… … … … … … ….*
*… … … … … ….. love,*
*… … … … … … ….. trust,*
*… … … … … … … ….. hope*
*Ground into the dirt*
*By muddy boots… … … … … ….*
*Groping… … … … … ….*
*For a view … … … … … …*
*… … … … … ….from the summit*
*… … … … … … …..Of pleasure,*
*… … … … … … … … … …. Pain*
*… … … … … … … futility.*

*Enduring … … … … … …*
*… … … … … … … …the pressure points*
*Of compromise*
*Withstanding… … … … … …*
*… … … … … … … …. the frigid breezes*
*Of unattended dreams*
*Fighting off … … … … … … … ….*
*the beleaguered beasts*
*… … … … … … … ….Of crushed hope*
*… … … … … … … …of buried talents*
*Waiting … … … … … … … …..*
*… … … … … … … … …for the Calvary charge*
*That will rescue… … … … … … … … ….*
*… … … … … … … … … … … … your fallen soul*
*From the imminent massacre at hand.*

*The enemy is not… … … ….*

*……………red-skinned*
*…………………savage*
*……………… nor evil*
*the enemy is not…….*
*……………A stranger*
*……………ignorant*
*……………or even mean.*
*They are ………………*
*……………Your confidents*
*………………your friends*
*……………..your family*
*………your loved ones*
*the ones you ………………..*
*would ………………*
*……………do anything for*
*accept………………..*
*……………… anything from*
*………………….die for*
*and even worse………..*
*……………………live for.*

*The saddest part…….*
*Of the battle……*

*You have them ……*
*In your sites…..*
*And your finger……*
*Is on the trigger.*

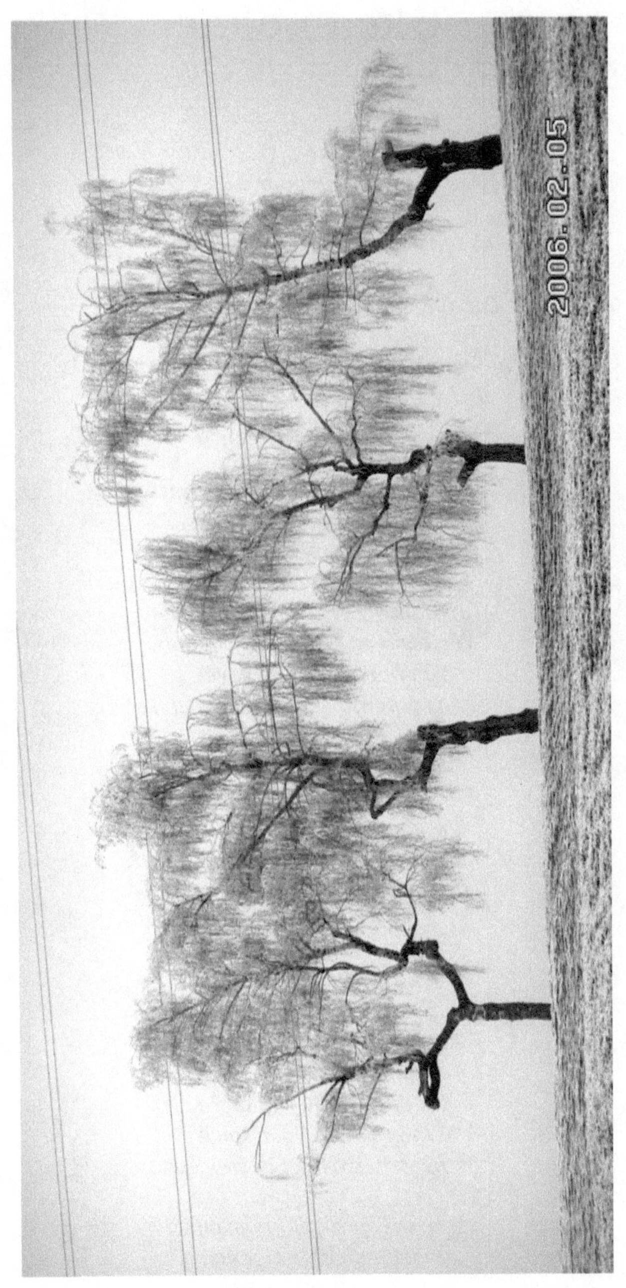
2006.02.05

# Okefenokee

*Flutter away... ......? or..*
*are you on your way?*
*Toward some horizon?*
*Away from a setting sun?*

*Landing on the upper-most-pinnacle*
*of the grandest edifice*
*in the worst meteorological conditions*
*under the most dire circumstances*

*Folding your wings*
*You face the torrential winds*
*What are you hoping to see?*
*Or are you wanting to BE seen?*

*You utter a single searching note*
*You echo an alluring symphony*
*You hope, trust, believe....*
*that a response exists in the depths.*

*It is the nature of wings*
*to seek out the heights,*
*Okefenokee drives your quest*
*toward the heavenly hands of peace.*

*There is no way ....*
*... .....to be sure*
*no positive proof.....*
*.....of existence.*
*But the question is rooted....*
*...deep in your heart and soul.*
*Not planted by you there...*
*In grown in your spirit*
*...at the very moment of conception.*

*Like the spark of life itself....*
*....the indelible signature*
*... .....of the Creator.*

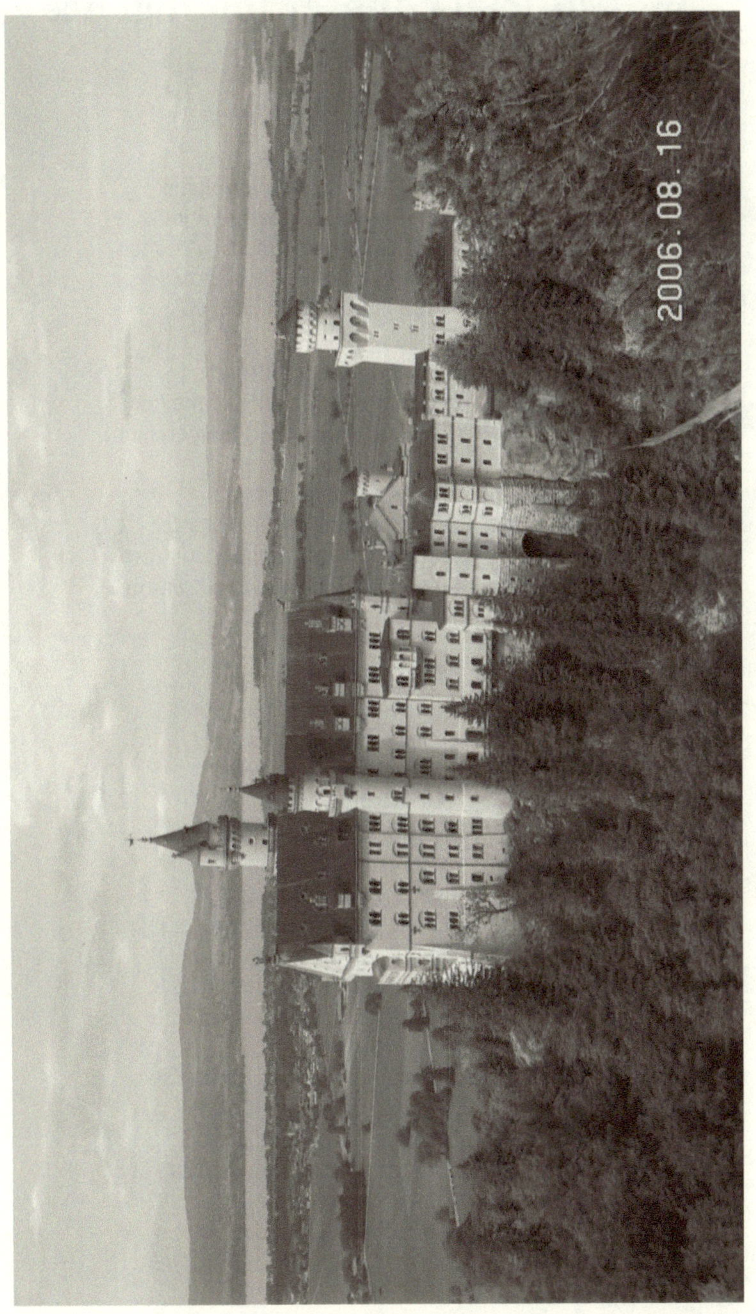
2006.08.16

# Artificial Counter Intelligence

It is not in my ambition
I no longer possess any,
To scale the mocking mountains
To swim the deepest perplexities
To challenge the enlightenment of the sun
Or expose the ineptitude of greed
Across the great deceptual divide.

The furniture of truth
Can be arranged to suit the lady of the house.
According the temptations and temperament
Of the times at hand.
It does not change much
But the perceptions of the observer
Can make them appear in direct contrast
To the attended configuration and reason.

The illumination used
Can throw shadows of doubt..
Hopeless and indispensable
Cuttingly crystallized..
Or hopelessly vague.

Who controls the light and breath
Of the seekers of the grail?
Information can be power
Or our penance for greed..
Leading us to wisdom
Or pushing us into oblivion.

Information does not lead..
To knowledge, truth, grace
Enslaving us in complex caves
Of unprocessable erroneous data
That will mire us is
Catatonic doubt and indecision.

The true capabilities of individuals
Are snared in an avalanche of random data
That cannot be sorted nor escaped from.
It buries our spirits in ash and cinder.

In our quest to make a machine
To imitate our minds
WE have created a mind
That imitates our machines.

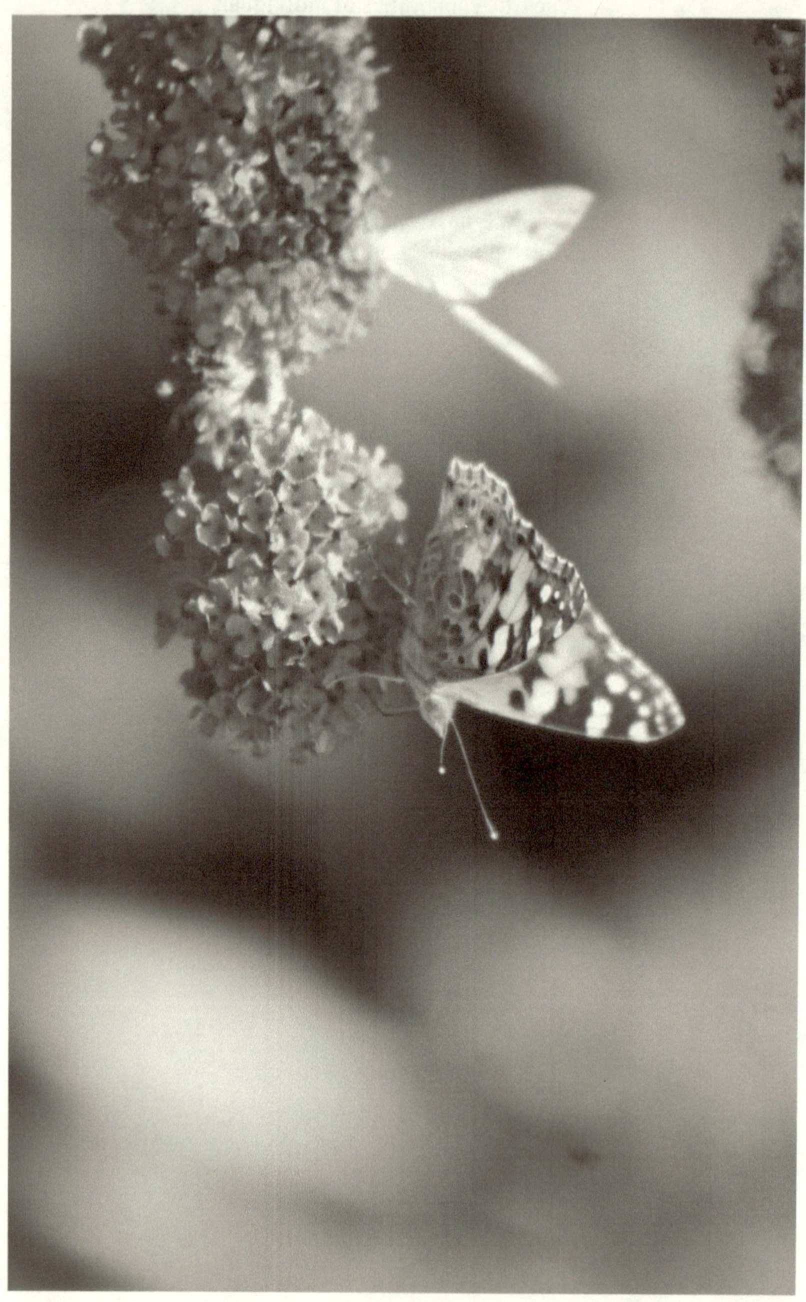

# *Obiwan*

whispering wisps cross my thoughts
*sirus nimbus filtered rays breech the breeze*
*hazy fragments of restless doubts*
*neglected ropes of hope whips of dingy dreams*
*gaze toward extinguished enlightenments*
*blinded teetering truth trips*
*chins fall on empty chiselled chests*

*crimson cardinals correspond in petrified pines*
*a frog follows in the bog*
*jiminy Cricket's feet play footsy*
*as the sun squats down in the west*
*preparing to spring day elsewhere*
*I open my eyes ,close my mind*
*To faults and losses.*

*Awful unlawful desires*
*Hold a knife to your character*
*Threatening to cut your monsters loose*
*Unleashing you and yours*
*On all dreams, hopes and exemplar example*
*Creating chaos corruption and despair*
*Where Bambi and butterflies play and breed.*

*Desire cannot define reality*
*Jedi masters mould them*
*Into oblique forms of logic and responsibility*
*desire tries to lop off the logical tentacles of restraints*
*using quick honest thrusts with his sabre of light*
*alas they reappear faster than the jedi can lance them*

*in the end the padawan is entangled*
*he must submit or join the Dark side*
*the place of no return or options*
*extinguish the light sabre, pledge allegiance*
*reality releases it's death grip*
*allowing the jedi access to the Force*
*that keeps the universe ordered and disciplined.*

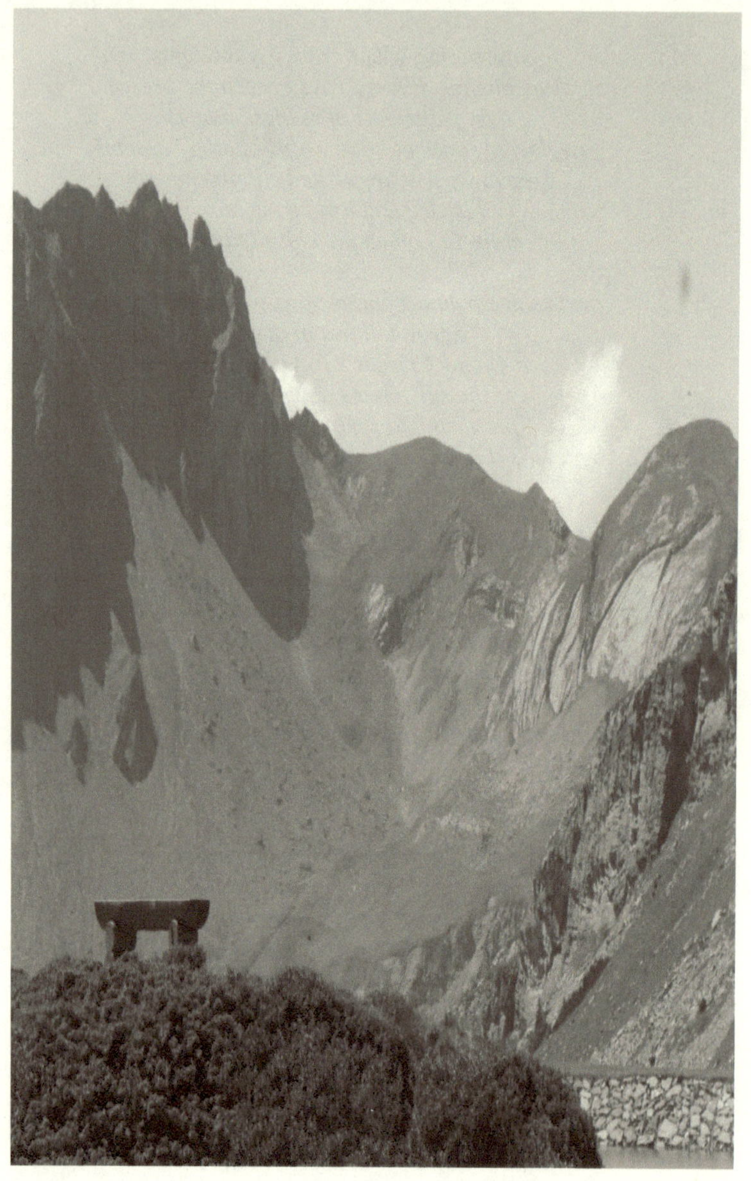

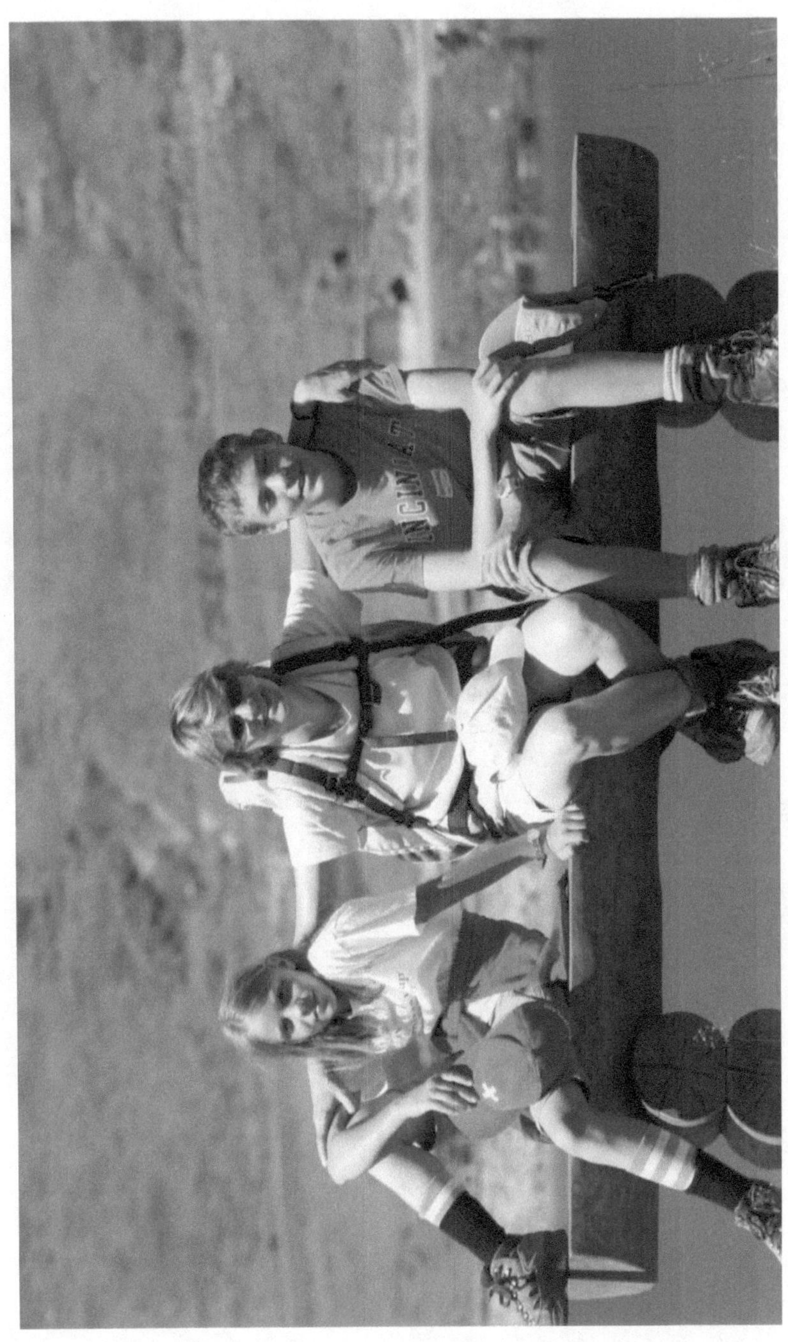

*A good day is a day…….*
*when we are more proud of the things*
*we have done,*
*then ashamed of the things*
*we have not done.*

www.ingramcontent.com/pod-product-compliance
Lightning Source LLC
LaVergne TN
LVHW091642100826
845152LV00006B/135/J

* 9 7 8 0 9 7 9 0 1 1 0 9 2 *